ESSAYS IN INTERNATIONAL FINANCE

No. 199, August 1996

MAKING EMU HAPPEN
PROBLEMS AND PROPOSALS: A SYMPOSIUM

PETER B. KENEN, EDITOR
JOHN ARROWSMITH, PAUL DE GRAUWE, CHARLES A. E. GOODHART,
DANIEL GROS, LUIGI SPAVENTA, AND NIELS THYGESEN

INTERNATIONAL FINANCE SECTION

DEPARTMENT OF ECONOMICS
PRINCETON UNIVERSITY
PRINCETON, NEW JERSEY

INTERNATIONAL FINANCE SECTION
EDITORIAL STAFF

Peter B. Kenen, *Director*
Margaret B. Riccardi, *Editor*
Lillian Spais, *Editorial Aide*
Lalitha H. Chandra, *Subscriptions and Orders*

Library of Congress Cataloging-in-Publication Data

Making EMU happen : problems and proposals : a symposium / Peter B. Kenen, editor
... [et al.].
    p. cm. — (Essays in international finance, ISSN 0071-142X ; no. 199)
    Includes bibliographical references.
    ISBN 0-88165-106-0 (pbk.) : $8.00
    1. Monetary policy—European Union countries—Congresses. 2. Monetary unions—
European Union countries—Congresses. I. Kenen, Peter B., 1932— . II. Series.
HG136.P7 no. 199
[HG930.5]
332.4'94—dc20   96-21195
                                                                           CIP

Printed in the United States of America by Princeton University Printing Services at Princeton, New Jersey

International Standard Serial Number: 0071-142X
International Standard Book Number: 0-88165-106-0
Library of Congress Catalog Card Number: 96-21195

CONTENTS

FIGURE

INTRODUCTION

Peter B. Kenen

In December 1995, the European Council, meeting in Madrid, confirmed "unequivocally" that the third and final stage of economic and monetary union (EMU) will begin on January 1, 1999. The Council chose "euro" as the name of the new single currency and adopted a timetable for decisions and actions that must be taken before and after the 1999 deadline. Nevertheless, difficult issues must still be resolved.

Early in 1998, as soon as the necessary data are available, the European Commission and European Monetary Institute (EMI) must report to the Council of Ministers on the degree of convergence achieved by each member of the European Union (EU), using the so-called convergence criteria set out in the Treaty on European Union (the "Maastricht Treaty"). The Council of Ministers must then decide which members fulfill the "necessary conditions for the adoption of a single currency" (that is, for joining the monetary union at the beginning of 1999).

At the start of the monetary union, the participating countries, commonly called the "Ins" or "insiders," must adopt irrevocably fixed exchange rates for their currencies and corresponding conversion rates between their currencies and the euro. At that same time, moreover, the European Monetary System (EMS) will cease to exist in its present form, and new arrangements may then be required to govern the behavior of exchange rates between the euro and the currencies of the nonparticipants, called the "Outs" or "outsiders."

Because these matters are being discussed intensively by officials and academic economists, and important decisions will probably be taken before the end of 1996, I invited a small group of economists to write short papers on these issues. The economists were asked to comment on one or more of the following questions:

(1) How should the convergence criteria be interpreted, especially the exchange-rate and fiscal criteria, which are not simply numerical? If very few countries can meet the criteria in 1998, should the start of the monetary union be delayed?

(2) How can the locking of exchange rates best be accomplished to minimize turbulence in the foreign-exchange market before and after the beginning of the monetary union?

1

(3) Should there be a formal successor to the EMS, to stabilize exchange rates between the currencies of the insiders and outsiders? If so, what form should it take, and should every outsider be obliged to join it?

Those invited to contribute to this symposium have written other papers on these issues, and they were encouraged to draw on their earlier work. That may be why all of them agreed to contribute, despite a demanding deadline. But readers who are familiar with the previous papers will still want to read what is written here, because the authors have taken account of the most recent developments. The contributors, whose papers appear in alphabetical order, are:

John Arrowsmith, Senior Research Fellow of the National Institute of Economic and Social Research in London and Director of its research program on European monetary and financial integration. Arrowsmith has also served as Senior Advisor on European Affairs at the Bank of England (1985–1994), Alternate Member of the Monetary Committee of the European Community (EC) and Member of the Alternates' Committee of the Committee of EC Central Bank Governors/EMI Council.

Paul De Grauwe, Professor of Economics at the University of Louvain and Fellow of the Centre for Economic Policy Research (CEPR). De Grauwe is the author of *The Economics of Monetary Integration* (1994), now in its second edition, and has written extensively on the transition to EMU. He is a member of the Belgian parliament.

Charles A.E. Goodhart, Professor of Economics and Deputy Director of the Financial Markets Group at the London School of Economics. Goodhart is the author of *Money, Information and Uncertainty* (1989) and *The Central Bank and the Financial System* (1995), and a coauthor of *The Future of Central Banking* (1994).

Daniel Gros, Deputy Director of the Centre for European Policy Studies (CEPS) in Brussels. Gros is the author of *Towards Economic and Monetary Union* (1996), the report of a CEPS Economic Policy Group, and coauthor, with Niels Thygesen, of *European Monetary Integration* (1992). He has also written several papers on the links between fiscal policies and monetary union.

Luigi Spaventa, Professor of Economics at the University of Rome, "La Sapienza," and Fellow of the Centre for Economic Policy Research (CEPR). Spaventa served as Minister of the Budget in Italy from 1993 to 1994. He is the author of numerous articles and essays.

2

Niels Thygesen, Professor of Economics at the University of Copenhagen and Associate Senior Fellow of the Centre for European Policy Studies (CEPS). Thygesen is the coauthor, with Daniel Gros, of *European Monetary Integration* (1992) and has written a number of papers on EMU. He was a member of the Delors Committee, of which the *Report on Economic and Monetary Union in the European Community* was the forerunner of the plan for EMU in the Maastricht Treaty.

A consolidated set of references has been placed at the end of the symposium.

THE ROLE OF EXCHANGE-RATE ARRANGEMENTS IN PREPARING FOR EMU

John Arrowsmith

At its meeting in Madrid on December 15 and 16, 1995, the European Council established what may be the definitive timetable for the move to economic and monetary union (EMU) within the framework of the Maastricht Treaty. Which European Union (EU) members will qualify to take part will be decided "as early as possible in 1998," and the third stage of EMU will begin on January 1, 1999, when exchange rates between the participant countries will be fixed irrevocably and a European currency, the "euro," will be used by the European System of Central Banks (ESCB) in its monetary-policy operations with the national banking systems. By July 1, 2002, the euro will have replaced the national currencies for all purposes. The Madrid meeting also reached agreement on many of the steps that will need to be taken between the start of the third stage and the emergence of the euro as the single currency two and a half years later. It did not, however, address a number of equally important issues that must be resolved during the two and a half years before Stage 3 begins.

Several of these issues concern the nature of exchange-rate relations among the fifteen members of the European Union, a matter on which the Maastricht Treaty gives little guidance. The test of exchange-rate stability, which a country must meet for two years before it may join the monetary union, is expressed in the Treaty in terms of participation in the exchange-rate mechanism (ERM) of the European Monetary System (EMS). The disruption that the ERM has undergone since the Treaty was signed, however, means that this is no longer an adequate test. Although it is now known approximately when the countries eligible to participate in the monetary union will be named and when the conversion rates for their currencies and for the euro will be irrevocably fixed, it is not yet known how the conversion rates will be chosen and how the participants' exchange rates might be managed in the six to eight months between the naming of countries and the fixing of rates. Decisions must also be made about the framework, if any, within which orderly exchange-rate relations might be governed after January 1, 1999, between the participants of the monetary union (the

4

insiders) and those EU members that are obliged temporarily to remain outside the union or that exercise their option to do so (the outsiders). Failure to resolve these issues soon could provoke uncertainty and destabilizing speculation and thus put at risk the smooth transition to monetary union.

1   The Exchange-Rate Criterion

The Maastricht Treaty (Article 109j[1]) lays down two "structural" tests of economic convergence: price stability and the absence of an excessive government deficit, and two "market" tests: the level of long-term interest rates and the maintenance of exchange-rate stability. The exchange-rate test is defined in terms of a country's observance of the "normal fluctuation margins" of the ERM, without devaluing and without severe tensions, for at least two years before the EMU entry examination, which, under the Madrid timetable, will be conducted by both the European Commission and the European Monetary Institute (EMI) in the first few months of 1998. When Article 109j was drafted, it was clearly understood to mean that a country would need to maintain the exchange rate for its currency against the currencies of other EU member states within what was then the "narrow band" of ±2¼ percent, as distinct from the "wide band" of ±6 percent, while also allowing that a decision might subsequently be taken to reduce the width of the narrow band *de jure*. In August 1993, the 2¼ and 6 percent bands were "temporarily" suspended in favor of a single band of ±15 percent, permitting the exchange rates of all ERM currencies to move against each other by up to 30 percent compared with the maximum of 4½ percent envisaged at the time of Maastricht.

Having already lasted two and a half years, this "temporary" arrangement might now be regarded as "normal," but it would be disingenuous to suggest that it provides a test of exchange-rate stability consistent with the spirit of the Treaty. So far, however, there has been no official guidance on whether or how the original formulation should be reinterpreted in the light of changed circumstances. The EMI Council gave a formal opinion in October 1994, subsequently endorsed by the ECOFIN Council (the Council of Ministers when attended by the ministers of economics and finance), which only ventured that, in the light of experience since the widening of the ERM bands and in the current circumstances, "the EMI considers it advisable to maintain the current arrangements" and that member states will be "contributing to fulfillment" of the convergence requirements if they aim at avoiding significant exchange-rate fluctuations by pursuing price stability and the reduction of fiscal deficits (EMI, 1995a). The Commission has made no formal pronouncement.

For those who question the economic logic behind the original decision to include a test of exchange-rate stability among the convergence criteria—whether as an indication of a country's sustained commitment to sound money policies, of its ability to adjust to asymmetric shocks without undue pain, or of the appropriate conversion rates at which currencies would be fixed irrevocably—the simplest solution to the problem could be to establish *de jure* that the temporary widening of the ERM fluctuation band to ± 15 percent is now permanent.[1] The operational content of the participation requirements for monetary union would then be reduced to a formal commitment by a country to maintain its currency within these much more generous limits, without having recourse to extreme policy actions or a devaluation of its central rate in order to achieve this. The necessary legal basis could be provided either by a resolution of the European Council, together with a decision by the EMI Council amending the original Central Bank agreement of March 1979, or by an amendment to the Treaty. This solution, however, is unlikely to find political acceptance. The failure of the Commission, the EMI, and the Council to clarify the criterion reflects a continuing disagreement between those member states that wish to retain a rigorous and formal test of exchange-rate stability and those that believe recent market experience shows that a more flexible framework is needed if the criterion is not to be self-defeating.

The need to resolve this conflict is now pressing. The clock must be started now if the criterion is to be met, in accordance with the Treaty, throughout the two years prior to the 1998 assessment of which countries qualify for monetary union in 1999. Furthermore, Article 109j(1) of the Treaty requires that the Commission and the EMI report to the ECOFIN Council which countries meet the four convergence criteria in time for ECOFIN and a special meeting of the Council of Ministers consisting of the heads of state or government to decide by the end of 1996 whether it will be appropriate to move to Stage 3 before January 1, 1999. Each of these bodies may be tempted to set aside its responsibilities under the Treaty to make such judgments this year. To do so, however, might be unwise. Failure to follow the required procedures because of an unfavorable conjuncture would set an unfortunate precedent. Token reports and decisions that shy away from the basic

---

[1] See, for example, Kenen, 1995b. A case for dropping all of the convergence criteria is made by De Grauwe, 1994b.

questions would be equally unsatisfactory. The markets will almost certainly be looking this year for guidance as to how the convergence criteria—and especially the two-year exchange-rate requirement—will be applied in 1998. Evasion or obfuscation at this time would only exacerbate the inevitable uncertainties ahead of the 1998 decision. A compromise solution to the problem of the ERM criterion is therefore urgently needed.

One approach might be to combine an *ex ante* requirement of two years of formal participation in the present 15 percent band and the achievement of a reasonable degree of stability, to be defined *ex post*, within the band. Such a retrospective assessment may be all that is possible for the Commission and EMI reports this year, but to leave open the definition of exchange-rate stability until the definitive assessments must be made in early 1998 would be both unfair and unwise; it could result in arbitrary and politically motivated judgments as to which currencies have or have not satisfied the criterion and in destabilizing speculation in financial markets beforehand about which countries might ultimately qualify. It would be wiser to establish now, or during the process of preparing the 1996 reports, a mutually acceptable definition of stability against which the performance of currencies participating in the ERM should be judged in 1998. This test might be "hard-edged" or "rounded."

In its hard-edged form, an exchange-rate band would be chosen, in a much narrower range than the 15 percent band, within which each currency would have to remain continuously (without severe strains) in order to qualify. A range of about ±2¼ percent around existing central rates would be broadly equivalent to a reintroduction of the narrow band without compulsory intervention obligations or unlimited short-term financing facilities. In present market circumstances, however, a somewhat wider band of, say, 5 or 6 percent would be more prudent. A number of other decisions would also have to be made that would affect the degree of symmetry inherent in the test: whether the bands should be defined in terms of the rates of participating currencies against the ECU or against each other; whether only the lower limit would be binding or whether in some circumstances a country under strong upward pressure might be required to choose between breaching its upper limit (thereby failing the test) or formally revaluing its ERM central rate (which would not constitute a violation of the criterion); and whether the band should be defined in relation to existing ERM central rates or in relation to the market exchange rates at the starting date.

In its more "rounded" form, the band could be defined in terms of some moving average of actual exchange rates over a specified interval of time. A limit could be set for the coefficient of variation of any currency (that is, its standard deviation expressed as a proportion of its mean value or central rate), which would allow for temporary breaches of the limit, provided there were compensating movements away from the limit at other times (Johnson, 1994; Taylor, 1995). It would still have to be decided from the outset whether the standard deviations should be calculated in relation to the ECU or to each of the other participating currencies, and whether they should be calculated with reference to central or to market rates. It would also be necessary to decide the frequency and intervals at which the coefficient is calculated and whether or not the upper limit is binding. Depending on the precise specification chosen, this "rounded" test would not necessarily be any less rigorous than the hard-edged version, but it would be more forgiving of occasional, unsustained, flurries in foreign-exchange markets. It is possible that thinking within the Commission and the EMI is already moving in this direction. In its 1995 Convergence Reports, the Commission presents exchange-rate data for thirteen-week moving coefficients of variation against the ECU and the deutsche mark, and the EMI shows logarithmic first differences of standard deviations against the deutsche mark, using daily observations over each quarter (Commission, 1995; EMI, 1995b).

2 Approaches to the Irrevocable Fixing of Exchange Rates

On the basis of reports from the Commission and the EMI specifying which countries have achieved convergence, in particular by meeting the criteria mentioned above, the ECOFIN Council will assess, and the heads of state and government will confirm, "as early as possible" in 1998, and in any event before July 1, 1998, which member states qualify to join the monetary union. The Treaty further provides that the conversion rates between the participating currencies (including the euro) will be adopted by ECOFIN on January 1, 1999. There will thus be a period of at least six months during which it will be known which currencies will be locked together but not the rates at which they will be locked. This will provide a window for speculation in financial markets about what rates might be chosen, whether existing market cross-rates are appropriate or whether there might be a final realignment at the moment of locking, and what the implications are for the value of the ECU and, subsequently, the euro.

It may be argued that the considerable flexibility afforded by the 15 percent ERM band provides the best defense against destabilizing speculation, perhaps with additional help from a clear statement by ECOFIN, at the moment the participating countries are named, that there will be no realignment of the central rates of the participating currencies, and that the conversion rates to be adopted on January 1, 1999, will be the market exchange rates at that time (as suggested by Kenen, 1995). This approach, however, still leaves open the possibility that currencies could move against each other by between 15 and 30 percent within the ERM band (depending on their initial positions) at a time when there might still be political hurdles to be faced, such as parliamentary votes or referenda in accordance with national constitutional requirements. Movements on such a scale, which in effect would constitute a market-induced "final realignment," would not necessarily provide the best basis for a permanent union.

A different approach would be for ECOFIN to anticipate the "final realignment" of central rates by announcing in advance, as soon as possible after the participating countries have been named, the conversion rates at which the countries' currencies will be locked.[2] If these conversion rates are not greatly out of line with market rates at the time of the announcement, and the convergence assessments are credible, speculation should be stabilizing, driving market rates toward the conversion rates up to the moment of locking. Prior announcement of conversion rates would also offer two additional advantages. It would give the ECB and the national central banks time to finalize in advance the administrative systems for the redenomination of accounts from national currencies to euros and for the conversion of participating currencies that will need to be in place at the moment of locking. It would also provide an opportunity, free from last-minute pressures, to select relatively user-friendly conversion rates between national currencies and the euro (Kenen, 1995a, and Goodhart, 1996, who notes the importance of such rates for public acceptability of EMU).

An alternative way to encourage stabilizing speculation would be to announce in advance that the conversion rates will be determined by a market-based formula, such as the average of daily spot rates over the final three or six months of 1998 (Richards, 1995). This would allow a degree of flexibility, while increasingly locking into the market a particular set of rates, thus providing a reasonably stable bridge between the exchange rates on which convergence assessments had been made and

[2] The Treaty requires ECOFIN to consult with the European Central Bank (ECB), which will not have been established until "immediately after" July 1, 1998.

the conversion rates ultimately adopted. The conversion rates between national currencies and the euro that would result from such a process, however, would be unlikely to be particularly user friendly or to be known with sufficient precision in advance to assist in the preparations of the central banks.

Although either form of preannouncement might be useful in managing the transition, both appear to be ruled out by two technical restrictions on the conversion rates to be adopted, one imposed by the Treaty and the other by the European Council at Madrid (Arrowsmith, 1996.[3]

The Treaty requires that the conversion rates adopted among the national currencies and against the ECU do not in themselves change the value of the ECU relative to third currencies. The European Council has stated that the ECU will be converted to the euro at the rate of 1 to 1. Because there can be no certainty that the market rate for the ECU at the moment of fixing will be equal to the preannounced rate for the euro (or to the value of the ECU basket implicit in the preannounced cross-rates between national currencies), these two conditions might be violated. If the market rates among the participating currencies have not by then fully converged on the cross-rates implied by the preannounced conversion rates between those currencies and the euro, the adjustment in currency values entailed by the move from market rates to fixed conversion rates will create a discontinuity between the external market value of the ECU basket (derived from the external value of the constituent currency amounts) and the implied external value of the euro (derived from the external market of a participating currency and its preannounced euro conversion rate).[4] The value of the ECU basket, however, will be determined in part by any component currencies that are not taking part in the fixing, and the external value of the ECU could thus well differ from the implied external value of the euro *even if* the market values of all the participating currencies are completely convergent on the intended cross-rates.[5] Similarly, a preannounced formula cannot ensure that the

[3] The restrictions also make a "final realignment" at the time of locking difficult.

[4] The adoption of rates that differ from market rates would be tantamount to a realignment. In principle, changes that are exactly offsetting when weighted according to the currency composition of the ECU would be admissible, as with a "last-minute" realignment of the ERM parity grid to rates other than the current market rates. Such a precise outcome, however, would be unlikely either to arise fortuitously from the market configuration or to result from formal realignment negotiations.

[5] Again, however improbable, the market rates of nonparticipating currencies in the ECU basket might happen to be exactly those required to ensure continuity of value

10

restrictions will be met, because market rates for one or more of the currencies might still differ from the historical averages that will determine the conversion rates. If preannouncement in some form is seen as offering the best prospect for a smooth transition to locked currencies, it will therefore be sensible to remove these restrictions, which, although intended to ensure continuity, can stand in its way.

3 Exchange-Rate Arrangements for a Two-Tier EMU

It is now widely accepted that if the move to monetary union in Europe takes place on January 1, 1999, some EU member states will be either unable or unwilling to participate. The resulting two-tier EMU will represent a fundamental change in the economic and political structure of the European Union. Countries remaining outside EMU (the outsiders) will not be staying put in the present framework, which treats all member states on roughly equal terms: Stage 2 will be replaced by a Stage 3 in which the interests of the monetary union will be paramount and the economic and monetary policies of the participants (the insiders) will be dominant (Arrowsmith, 1995a). The exclusion of some member states from the monetary union could prove disruptive, not only to their own economies but also to the wider Single Market and, ultimately, to the fledgling monetary union itself. It is therefore essential to find a way to reconcile the needs of the participants with those of the nonparticipants. This can be done only within an agreed upon cooperative framework in which all member states assume mutual and reciprocal rights and obligations. With only two and a half years to design and install such a framework, the EMI and the ECOFIN Council are now beginning to address the issue.

One solution is already implicit in the Treaty—the continuation of the EMS and its exchange-rate mechanism. In its original, narrow-band form, this may be unacceptable to a number of member states, although for reasons that are more political than economic. Too much was expected of the mechanism initially, and not enough was required of the participants when faced with hard choices. In its present form, however, the ERM is probably too loose to meet future needs, and some rethinking of the basic design will be necessary to accommodate the new circumstances of a two-tier EMU. Nevertheless, the ERM

---

between the ECU and the euro, *or* the nonparticipating countries might conceivably be persuaded to realign their currencies at the last minute to accommodate the position of the participating countries.

could provide the basic elements of a cooperative solution: a nonrigid and adjustable exchange-rate framework, the coordination of monetary and exchange-rate policies, a set of rules governing intervention behavior, and temporary (and perhaps conditional) financing facilities. Each of these elements could be adjusted in ways that would safeguard the interests of the monetary union while providing a safety net for those outside the union and encouragement for them to pursue sound policies leading to economic convergence.

The precise form of the mechanism itself need not be identical to that of the original ERM. The "normal" fluctuation margins for the currencies of the more convergent outsiders could be made somewhat wider than ±2¼ percent at, say, 2½ percent. If the margins were set in relation to the euro, rather than against each participating currency in a multilateral grid, the currencies could move against the euro by a maximum of 5 percent and thus against each other by a maximum of 10 percent—more than double the movement available to them in the former narrow band, but only one-third the movement permitted by the current 15 percent band. The band could be either hard-edged, requiring spot rates against the euro to be maintained continuously within the band, or soft-edged, in terms of a moving average or standard deviation, as suggested above in the context of the exchange-rate stability test. The need for additional flexibility between the euro and the currencies of the less convergent outsiders (including subsequent new members) could be met by a second band allowing margins of, perhaps, ±6 percent against the euro. This would allow the same amount of movement between the less convergent outsider currencies and the euro as the original wide band of the ERM (12 percent), but twice as much flexibility (24 percent) against other outsider currencies.

The experience of 1992–93 has demonstrated the crucial importance of the nature of the intervention and financing obligations in such a scheme. The mutuality of unlimited reciprocal intervention and of multilateral financing with shared (ECU-denominated) foreign-exchange risk may have been appropriate to the single-tier Europe, but even then, it proved unsustainable. In a two-tier Europe, a more pragmatic arrangement is probably needed. Reciprocal intervention and automatic finance could be made available up to a pre-set limit, as exists now for intramarginal intervention.[6] Beyond that limit, further financing would

---

[6] Under the Basle-Nyborg Agreement of 1987, the limits for very short-term financing of intramarginal intervention for each country were set at 200 percent of its debtor quota in the Short-Term Monetary Support Facility (the "Soutien").

be available, subject to policy conditions, up to a ceiling to be determined on a case-by-case basis. One policy requirement might be that the outsider leave fully unsterilized any foreign-exchange-market intervention it might undertake, whereas the ECB would remain free to sterilize its own interventions (Thygesen, 1996). A given amount of intervention to defend the currency of an outsider, however, would be more modest in relation to the monetary union as a whole than (as before) in relation to the German economy alone, and a repayment obligation in euros rather than in ECUs would place the exchange risk implied by devaluation entirely on the shoulders of the devaluing country.

A clearly articulated arrangement of this kind might still prove politically unacceptable to some member states, and obligatory participation by outsiders in a reformulated ERM would be contrary to both the existing EMS agreement and the Maastricht Treaty. For countries unwilling to participate in the new ERM, or for which the economies are not yet sufficiently integrated, a looser framework might be devised to exercise restraint on unfettered floating. This might take the form of a mutual code of conduct, the details of which would be laid down in secondary EU legislation. Adherence could be voluntary in the strict legal sense, although there would be a strong expectation (as with the EMS at present) that all member states would subscribe—and adherence would be a prior condition for participation in the narrow band and hence a precondition for later entry to the monetary union.

Such a code would establish principles according to which the exchange-rate policies of both the ECB and the outsiders would be conducted and a framework of rules defining permissible degrees of exchange-rate movement between the euro and outsider currencies, beyond which countervailing monetary-policy (and perhaps other economic-policy) action would be taken. Guidelines would also be set for the use by one country of another country's currency or of the euro in foreign-exchange intervention, and multilateral financing facilities could be made available subject to economic-policy conditions. These arrangements would be underpinned by more active multilateral surveillance of economic performance and policies, in accordance with the existing provisions of the Treaty and the continuing objective of convergence. In this context, the ECB and the outsiders might adopt a common inflation target but with different time frames for achieving it.

With a code setting a basic standard for the conduct of orderly exchange-rate relations among all members of the Single Market and a reformulated ERM providing a graduated approach to membership in the monetary union, other optional and more closely drawn arrange-

13

ments could be added to suit the needs of particular member states. It has been suggested, for example, that a currency-board relation with the euro might be appropriate for Denmark (Thygesen, 1996), whereas a country such as Italy might be offered associate membership in the monetary union. Under associate membership, Italy would have a completely fixed exchange rate but no voting rights in the ECB until the fall in Italian interest rates (prompted by membership) had brought about a sufficient improvement in Italian government finances (Gros, 1995a). Whether or not such subordinate relationships would prove politically acceptable, however, a multiplicity of special arrangements might give confusing signals to financial markets and compromise the basic structure proposed above.

4 A Synthesis

The foregoing analysis identifies three successive phases in the transition to monetary union during which a more rigorous framework than that of the present ERM may be needed to ward off speculative pressures and to promote orderly exchange-rate relations among the member states. Various proposals have been made to address the particular requirements of each stage. Just as a great variety of arrangements for outsiders might prove confusing and even counterproductive, so might a quick succession of different exchange-rate arrangements as the Maastricht timetable unfolds. What is needed, rather, is a strong cord of continuity running through all three phases, so that the main elements of the framework required in 1999 are in place now, when the trial period for exchange-rate stability must begin.

The first of these elements, on which agreement should be relatively easy, should be a code of conduct to which all member states can subscribe. The second should be a formal *ex ante* definition of exchange-rate stability. This could be used in the assessments of convergence in early 1998. It could also provide the basis for a narrower band within the ERM that could serve as a bridge to the locking of exchange rates on January 1, 1999, and after that, as an exchange-rate arrangement for countries that expect to join the monetary union a little later. In addition, a preannounced averaging formula for determining the conversion rates could be designed and made compatible with such a definition. For these various purposes, it would be advisable for the definition to be quite narrowly drawn but to be given soft edges of the kind described above. The outer limits of the ERM could be modified at the same time to meet the future needs of a two-tier EMU, although it might be wiser to adjust them only when Stage 3 starts. At that point, unless the ECU or some similar official basket of EU currencies is allowed to continue, the nature of the ERM itself will change radically, from a multilateral parity grid to a set of bilateral parities expressed in euros, with a corresponding change in the computation of the fluctuation margins. The code of conduct surrounding the ERM and the newly defined narrow band within it would provide a valuable degree of continuity when that change occurs.

REFORMING THE TRANSITION TO EMU

Paul De Grauwe

1   The Dynamics of Convergence toward EMU

The Maastricht Treaty has set out a blueprint for moving the members of the European Union (EU) into an economic and monetary union (EMU). The striking aspect of the Maastricht strategy is that countries are asked to provide evidence of good macroeconomic behavior before they are allowed to join the monetary union. They are required to satisfy convergence criteria with regard to inflation rates, long-term interest rates, stable exchange-rates, and fiscal policies.

The idea that countries should satisfy standards of good macroeconomic behavior is surprising on two counts. First, no previous attempt at creating a monetary union has followed such a strategy. The German monetary unification of 1990, the most recent example, did not use this approach. If it had done so, the monetary union between East and West Germany would not have occurred. Second, traditional economic theory concerning the conditions necessary for membership in a monetary union (the theory of optimum currency areas) lists none of the macroeconomic conditions delineated at Maastricht. It stresses, instead, microeconomic conditions that should be fulfilled, which may be summarized as follows:[1] When countries are different in economic structure, they are likely to face asymmetric shocks. If unable to use the exchange-rate instrument, they will need substantial flexibility in their labor markets (wage flexibility, for example, or labor mobility) in order to adjust to these shocks and to prevent them from leading to permanent unemployment. According to traditional theory, therefore, the conditions for a successful monetary union are microeconomic in nature. They have nothing to do with the macroeconomic conditions specified at Maastricht.

The theory of optimum currency areas also stresses the need for budgetary flexibility, rather than adherence to strict limits on budget

[1] The *loci classici* are Mundell (1961), McKinnon (1963), and Kenen (1969). For a recent survey, see Tavlas (1994). This theory has also led to a burgeoning empirical literature. See, for example, Neumann and von Hagen (1994), Bayoumi and Eichengreen (1993), and De Grauwe and Vanhaverbeke (1993).

16

deficits (Bayoumi and Masson, 1994). Because countries that enter a monetary union will lose an important instrument of economic policy—their ability to set national monetary policies—they may need to use fiscal policies more intensively when they face asymmetric shocks. National fiscal policies should therefore be allowed to diverge, at least temporarily, from the unionwide average. A failure to allow countries to pursue divergent fiscal policies will put more pressure on the European Central Bank (ECB) to do something about these shocks. According to traditional theory, too little fiscal flexibility may endanger the stability of monetary policymaking at the union level.

If the Maastricht convergence criteria have nothing to do with the conditions necessary to make a workable monetary union in Europe, how can they be justified economically? The need for convergence criteria has been defended on two grounds. First, they are thought to be necessary to guarantee that the future monetary union will produce low inflation. This assertion has been made with regard to both the inflation criterion and the budgetary criteria. Second, the budgetary-convergence criteria (the 3 percent budget-deficit rule and the 60 percent government-debt norm) are thought to be necessary to avoid spillover effects of fiscal policies from one country to others. These spillover effects are deemed to be more pronounced inside than outside the union and to threaten its stability. Regulations on budgetary policies are thus seen as a means to guarantee stability of the monetary union. These claims are analyzed below in more detail.

Convergence Criteria and Monetary Stability in EMU

The argument that the inflation criterion is necessary to guarantee low inflation in EMU may be phrased as follows. Countries have different inflation reputations. Germany, for example, has established a reputation of low inflation; Italy has acquired a less favorable reputation. When these two countries form a monetary union, the union's own reputation will reflect an average of Germany's and Italy's reputations. As a result, the union's inflation rate is likely to be higher than the rate observed in Germany but lower than the rate in Italy. Clearly, EMU could live with that. The problem is that Germany would be unhappy with this outcome, because it would have to accept a higher inflation rate. It would therefore insist that EMU's average inflation rate not exceed the German rate and would very likely make Germany's participation conditional on this outcome.

The inflation-convergence criterion can now be understood as a mechanism that requires Italy to establish a more favorable inflation

17

reputation prior to entering EMU. Italy should do this outside the union, by reducing its inflation rate on its own. If this is costly, so much the better, because it will show that the Italian authorities are willing to change their priorities to acquire a better reputation. Once Italy has achieved this, it may be admitted to the union without tarnishing the reputation of the other participants. The monetary union can then develop into a low-inflation zone.

A similar argument can be developed to justify the budgetary norms. The authorities of countries with high government debt ratios have incentives to create a surprise inflation so as to reduce the real burden of government debt. If these countries are accepted into the union, they will push for higher inflation rates than countries with lower debt ratios will support, thereby increasing the union's average inflation rate. In order to avoid this outcome, the high-debt countries will have to reduce their debt ratios before entering the union.[2] An argument can thus be made for imposing prior convergence of inflation and government debt ratios to ensure that the future monetary union will exhibit low rates of inflation.

The first point to note in this regard is that the convergence criteria provide no guarantee of lower inflation in the future monetary union. The convergence dynamics may be seen as a game in which countries are rewarded for following a painful disinflationary policy and punished—that is, excluded from the monetary union—for failing to reduce inflation. Countries therefore have strong incentives to comply with the criteria by adopting disinflationary strategies—those countries, at least, that deem the permanent benefits of joining EMU to exceed the temporary costs of the disinflationary strategy. Once these countries are admitted to EMU, however, the nature of the game, that is, its reward-and-punishment structure, changes fundamentally, because the punishment suddenly vanishes. This change must have important effects on countries' behavior. Those countries that initially were "softer" on inflation are likely to exhibit the same preferences within EMU. One may argue that the convergence process required prior to entry may have changed their preferences and converted them permanently to low-inflation policies, but this is a tenuous assumption. It is more realistic to assume that these countries will revert to their prior preferences. The convergence criteria do not, in themselves, guarantee low inflation in the future. Such a guarantee can come only from the

---

[2] Note that this does not establish the need for the numbers 3 (budget deficit) and 60 (GDP ratio), the arbitrariness of which has been justly criticized (Buiter, Corsetti, and Roubini, 1993).

nature of the institutions that will be set up under EMU. I shall return to this issue later.

The fact that the convergence criteria cannot ensure low inflation under EMU has important implications for Germany and has led to strong pressures within Germany to postpone monetary union. For Germany, the costs and benefits of monetary union are asymmetric. The benefits consist of the usual gains from a monetary union (lower transactions costs, elimination of exchange-rate uncertainty, and avoidance of misalignments of exchange rates). The costs reside in the risk of higher future inflation. There is, however, another cost. When Germany enters the union, it loses its power to determine monetary conditions in Europe as a whole. In addition, abandoning the deutsche mark can be seen as abandoning a "brand name" that has been costly to establish. Both the loss of monetary hegemony in Europe and the loss of the brand name are costs incurred up front, at the start of the union. The benefits from EMU, however, are a yearly and uncertain return. This structure of costs and benefits creates a situation in which waiting has a positive value for Germany.[3]

Suppose Germany enters EMU on January 1, 1999. This implies an immediate and irreversible loss of power and brand name (the sunk costs) for Germany. Assume that the present value of the future net return from EMU exceeds this cost. One might think this a sufficient reason for Germany to enter the union on January 1, 1999, but this is unlikely to be the case. The yearly future return is uncertain. By waiting, say, two years, Germany may obtain more information about the commitment of the other potential members to low inflation, and therefore about the net return from EMU for Germany. If this return is high enough, the two-year wait implies a loss of only two years of return. If, instead, the return is low (because of a weak commitment to low inflation and low government debt by the other members), Germany will have avoided the large up-front cost. Germany thus sees a positive value in waiting and so has a strong incentive to postpone the start of EMU.

One may object that Germany cannot decide to postpone the start of EMU, because the dates and procedures for beginning have been set in the Maastricht Treaty. The Treaty provides considerable leeway,

---

[3] It can be argued that other countries also face an asymmetric structure of costs and benefits, that they also lose their monetary-policy instrument when joining the union. The situation of these other countries is different, however, because most of them have already ceded monetary control to Germany. In addition, they do not face a similar brand-name loss when they abandon their respective currencies.

however, in interpreting these procedures. Take, for example, the debt-to-GDP ratio. According to the Treaty, the debt ratio should decline "sufficiently" and approach the 60 percent reference value at a "satisfactory pace." This wording was introduced to provide some flexibility, but it can also be used to argue for postponement. Most countries will not have reached the 60 percent reference value by January 1, 1999, and it will be possible to argue that the decline has been insufficient or has proceeded at an unsatisfactory pace. Waiting a little longer to see how the debt ratios evolve makes perfect sense to the German authorities, who attach considerable importance to the budget indicators as signals of a commitment to low inflation.

The convergence requirements can thus be seen to involve a dynamic that produces strong incentives to postpone the start of EMU. This dynamic, in turn, has important implications for the countries with weak reputations for monetary and budgetary stability.

The Dynamics of Convergence for Countries with Weak Reputations

The countries with weak reputations suffer from a double problem. Take the example of Italy (or, equally, Spain). If Italy is forced to reduce its inflation rate before entering the monetary union and must do so carrying the burden of a low reputation, economic agents will be skeptical, and inflationary expectations will not decline easily. The Italian authorities must therefore move the economy along a downward-sloping short-term Phillips curve and generate higher unemployment. The ultimate success of this strategy is not guaranteed. The Italian authorities may very likely fail to acquire an inflation reputation comparable to Germany's, in which case Italy will never quite reach the same low-inflation equilibrium. Because the Maastricht Treaty also requires Italy to peg its exchange rate, the lira will experience an increasing real appreciation during the transition, leading to doubts that the disinflationary process can be sustained. Speculative crises will then be set in motion, forcing devaluations of the lira and widening the divergence of inflation rates. To qualify for entry, Italy will have to start a new round of disinflation, which may begin again and again.

A similar problem arises with budgetary convergence. Consider countries with weak budgetary performance (Belgium, Italy, Sweden). As long as they are kept out of the monetary union, doubts will exist about their eventual entry. These doubts will also be fed by the knowledge that Germany has an incentive to postpone the start of the union (or to postpone the entry of these particular countries). As a result, devaluation risk will be built into the interest rates of the countries with high government debts and deficits. High long-term interest rates, moreover, will make it difficult for them to reduce the burden of the government debt. The fact that countries with weak public finances are kept outside the union will thus make their public finances worse and budgetary convergence all the more difficult.

The problem of budgetary convergence is made even worse in countries with poor inflation reputations. The real interest rate in these countries is likely to increase during the disinflation period, because the disinflationary strategy is not fully credible. The decline in observed inflation will therefore not be matched by a decline in expected inflation. As a result, the nominal interest rate does not decline apace with the decline in the observed inflation rate. Put differently, when disinflationary policies suffer from poor credibility, the *ex post* real interest rate is likely to increase, thereby also increasing the debt burden of the government.

All this creates doubts about the possibility of meeting the Maastricht targets and the potential for speculative crises that will, in turn, raise interest rates in countries with weak public finances. The troublesome aspect of these crises is that they may become self-fulfilling and thus validate doubts about the ability of these countries to meet the Maastricht criteria. The convergence process itself may therefore impede a quick reduction of inflation and budget deficits. If this is a correct characterization of the convergence dynamics for countries such as Italy, allowing these countries into the union without imposing prior convergence requirements would actually facilitate their convergence. In particular, it would make it easier for them to reduce their budget deficits and to start a program of debt reduction.

The dynamics of the Maastricht convergence criteria create a great risk of splitting the European Union apart. Some countries that find it difficult to converge in time to enter EMU on January 1, 1999, will also find it difficult to converge thereafter. The dynamics described above, which make convergence difficult for countries with a weak budgetary or inflationary reputation, will be at work after 1999 as well. As a result, those that are left out in 1999 may in fact be left out for a long time. Such a division in the European Union will create problems not only for the countries left out of EMU, but also for those that enter EMU from the start. The exchange rates between the euro and the outsider currencies are likely to be volatile, creating distortions in trade flows and undermining the Single Market. Instead of promoting integration, a two-speed Europe is likely to set back the existing level of economic integration.

This seems to be a paradox. On the one hand, Germany perceives the entry into the union of highly indebted countries such as Belgium, Italy, and Sweden to be against Germany's national interest, because the entry of these countries might jeopardize price stability in the future monetary union. On the other hand, letting these countries into the union would make it easier for them to reduce their inflation and government debt. Furthermore, allowing them in would eliminate the risk of a deep division in the European Union. The challenge today is how to resolve this paradox, how to reduce the risk of splitting the European Union while accommodating German fears of excessive inflation in the future. Several proposals for resolving this dilemma are considered below.

Budgetary Convergence Requirements and Spillover Effects

The previous sections discussed the convergence requirements as necessary devices to guarantee low inflation under EMU. The 3 percent and 60 percent budgetary norms were also defended as ways to prevent budget deficits and debt levels that would be large enough to create externalities (spillover effects) harmful to the other members of the union.[4] It is in the interest of all the member countries to prevent too high budget deficits and debt levels from arising in the first place, so as to avoid these negative externalities.

Where do these externalities originate? Several sources have been stressed. First, when a member of a monetary union borrows too heavily to finance budget deficits, it raises the interest rate in the monetary union and thereby increases the burden of debt in other member countries. Second, the higher interest rates produced by excessive borrowing by one member lead to crowding-out effects in the whole union. Third, when one member country issues too much government debt, the risk of default increases. If default occurs, the pressure on the other countries to bail out the defaulting government will be overwhelming. To avoid having to organize a costly bailout, the other governments have an interest in preventing a default from occurring by imposing Maastricht-like limits on budget deficits and government debt levels.

Although there is no question that the spillover effects of fiscal policies must be addressed in a monetary union, the importance of

---

[4] This view has been heavily criticized by, among others, Buiter, Corsetti, and Roubini (1993), who have insisted that the term "externality" is misplaced, and that the fiscal criteria have nothing to do with the concept of externalities used in economics.

these effects can easily be overestimated for several reasons. First, world capital markets are increasingly integrated, so that long-term real interest rates tend to be equalized.[5] Excessive borrowing by, say, the Italian authorities can therefore influence the real interest rate in the union only to the extent that it changes the world real interest rate. Italy (or any other future EMU member) is too small, however, to have an appreciable influence on the world real interest rate. The spillover effects on real interest rates within the future monetary union are thus likely to be small.

Second, capital markets are increasingly sophisticated. They are able to price the bonds issued by governments so as to allow for default risk. By consequence, the spillover effects are reduced. When one government increases its debt, the market will attach an appropriate risk premium to it, thereby insulating the debt issued by other governments. This also has the effect of putting the burden of the excessive debt on the issuing government itself.

Third, the risks of bailouts can be easily exaggerated. Two questions arise. Does the acceptance of a highly indebted country into the union increase the probability of default? And is the pressure to bail out a defaulting country greater when it is in the union than when it remains outside? Let us consider these two issues consecutively.

Proponents of tight budgetary conditions for entry have argued that the budgetary discipline inside a monetary union is looser than outside a union, because national member governments can borrow in a larger "domestic" capital market without incurring an exchange risk. They will then borrow too much, thereby increasing default risk. It must be admitted that the ability to borrow more without incurring exchange risk "softens" the government's budget constraints. There is, however, another feature of a monetary union that "hardens" the constraint. In a monetary union, there are several national governments and only one central bank. When entering the monetary union, the national governments have less direct access to a central bank than they had before they entered the union. The ability of each national government to finance a budget deficit by issuing money is therefore reduced considerably once it has entered a monetary union. As a result, the government's budget constraint becomes harder, reducing the incentive to run large budget deficits. It should be added that the reduced access to

---

[5] See Barro and Sala-i-Martin (1991), Obstfeld (1993), and Helbling and Wescott (1995), but also the contrary evidence of Feldstein and Horioka (1980). The consensus today is that the Feldstein-Horioka econometric evidence is not in contradiction with high capital mobility.

monetary financing will add to the incentive to issue more bonds. Nevertheless, it remains true that the hardening of the budget constraint should reduce the deficit and thus also reduce the net issue of government bonds.

When comparing these two effects (the larger access to borrowings free of exchange risk and the reduced possibility of monetary financing), it is unclear *a priori* which one will prevail. It is therefore also impossible to conclude that budgetary discipline becomes looser in a monetary union, requiring additional constraints on budget deficits and debts, so as to reduce the risk of default.[6]

Eichengreen and von Hagen (1995) have recently added another dimension to this discussion. They provide evidence that monetary union members that maintain control over a large domestic tax base face a lower default risk than do members that have smaller fiscal responsibilities. Because the European monetary union will consist of countries having large domestic taxing powers, the risk of default is likely to be small, compared to the risk faced by, say, the American states or Canadian provinces, which have limited taxing powers. Eichengreen and von Hagen conclude that the need to impose tight limits on government deficits because of possible default risks has been overemphasized in the context of EMU.

Does the risk of a bailout increase in a monetary union? The standard affirmative answer runs as follows. In a monetary union, financial integration increases. As a result, bonds issued by national authorities will be more widely distributed across member countries. A default by one member country will therefore affect more individuals and financial institutions outside the defaulting country than if the country had not been in the union, and more pressure will be exerted on other members to bail out the defaulting member.

Although it cannot be denied that the strong financial integration provided by a monetary union may generate considerable pressure to bail out defaulting governments, this is not the only relevant consideration. There is also the issue of exchange rates. Even if a country such as Italy is not allowed into EMU, an Italian default will still create considerable pressure on the other EU members to bail out the Italian government. If Italy is outside the monetary union when it defaults, the lira is likely to collapse, producing pressure from industrialists in the rest of the European Union to support the lira to spare them a loss of

---

[6] De Grauwe (1994a) and Moesen and Van Rompuy (1990), however, present some evidence that cutting the link between the central bank and the government does lead to lower debts and deficits.

competitiveness. This exchange-rate effect would be absent if Italy were to default after joining the monetary union. Keeping Italy outside the union may therefore not necessarily reduce the risk of a future bailout. The two effects, the financial-integration effect and the exchange-rate effect, operate in opposite directions. We simply do not know *a priori* whether the pressure to bail out a defaulting EU country will be stronger if the country is a member of EMU than if it is left outside the monetary union. It could very well be the other way around.

2 Alternative Transition Processes

The analysis in the previous sections suggests a number of reforms in the transition process to EMU. The transition to EMU should put less emphasis on convergence requirements and more on strengthening the monetary institutions of the future union. In other words, more emphasis should be put on ensuring that the future ECB provides price stability. If this can be done, the convergence criteria can be used more flexibly.

This general strategy could be implemented in several ways. Daniel Gros (1995) has proposed that countries that fail to satisfy the budgetary norms should be denied the right to vote in the Governing Council of the ECB. Countries such as Belgium, Italy, and Sweden would therefore be admitted into the monetary union, but they would not be allowed to take part in the decisionmaking process of the ECB until they had met the fiscal requirements. There would then be no reason to fear that heavily indebted countries might push the ECB to pursue lax monetary policies. This proposal would also resolve the paradox discussed earlier; if highly indebted countries are admitted into the union, it will be easier for them to meet their debt-reduction targets.

A second institutional reform would define and enforce a procedure for removing the members of the Governing Council of the ECB should the bank fail to maintain price stability. Such a procedure would do much more to ensure price stability in the monetary union in, say, the year 2010 than the insistence that countries reduce their inflation rates and their budget deficits in the second half of the 1990s, before the union starts. Such a reform would also go some way toward making the future ECB more accountable. Inflation targeting could be useful in this context. Many central banks now engage in inflation targeting. The ECB could be required to use it too.

The budgetary processes in the EU countries should also be reformed so as to make them more transparent and less prone to lead to unsustainable budget deficits. Eichengreen and von Hagen (1995) have recently formulated proposals aimed at streamlining the budgetary processes in the European Union. They have suggested, in addition, that a national debt board be established in each country to monitor the evolution of the national debt and to propose remedial action when particular targets are not met.

These are only a few of the proposals advanced to implement the general principle formulated earlier—that less emphasis should be put on the convergence criteria and more on the strengthening of the institutions of the future monetary union. It is important to see this as a *quid pro quo*. Stronger institutions might convince the German public that the future monetary union will provide low inflation, and Germany might then accept the relaxation of the convergence requirements (which provide few guarantees for Germany). Relaxation of the convergence criteria would in turn reduce the risk that the European Union will split into two parts, producing great economic and political strains.

It should be stressed that this shift in emphasis can be achieved within the framework of the Maastricht Treaty. As mentioned earlier, the wording of the Treaty allows for considerable flexibility in the interpretation of the convergence criteria, especially the budgetary criterion. If the political will is present, a flexible interpretation of the convergence requirements is certainly possible. At the same time, institutional strengthening can be achieved by negotiating additional protocols.

3 Problems in the Starting of EMU

Two important problems associated with the start of EMU deserve attention. First, because membership will be decided in early 1998 but Stage 3 will not begin until January 1, 1999, speculative crises may occur in the months preceding EMU. Second, because the national currencies will continue to circulate (albeit with irrevocably fixed exchange rates) during the three years (1999 to 2002) following EMU, speculative crises may arise in the months following EMU. How serious are these problems?

Conversion Rates and Speculation

Although the membership issue will be settled in early 1998 (if at all), the conversion rates for the members' currencies will not be known with certainty until January 1, 1999. Speculative crises may therefore arise, for either of two reasons. One is that large asymmetric shocks during 1998 will be perceived as creating a need for exchange-rate adjustments prior to the start of EMU, so as to avoid locking rates at values that no longer correspond to equilibrium. A second may result from what has been called the "end-game" problem. At the start of Stage 3, countries lose their ability to change their exchange rates. They may therefore want to devalue their currencies for the last time just before exchange rates are locked. A country that decides to devalue can reap the benefits of such a devaluation (for example, improved competitiveness, reduction of the real burden of the government debt) without creating expectations of another devaluation in the future— expectations that typically raise domestic interest rates and make a devaluation less attractive. The incentive to devalue "for the last time" may thus be very strong in a number of countries, and a speculative crisis is likely to erupt when speculators become aware of it.

How important are these problems? Let us examine the "end-game" problem first. When countries are selected to enter EMU in the beginning of 1998, they will have to comply with Article 109l of the Treaty, which says that the decision concerning the permanent conversion rates must be taken by unanimity. In other words, at the moment a country is accepted into EMU, it will abandon its sovereignty over its exchange rate. This eliminates the end-game problem. Devaluation will not be an option for countries that enter the union.[7]

The other problem, the possible occurrence of large shocks during 1998, cannot be excluded. The issue is how the participating countries should deal with the problem. One possible response would be to announce the conversion rates simultaneously with the membership decision. Such an announcement, however, must be made credible so as to withstand a speculative storm should one arise. A "commitment technology" should therefore be put in place. This would consist of steps toward the centralization of the monetary policies of the countries that will participate in EMU. The policies of these countries should be agreed upon from the date on which the countries are accepted, and each country should declare that its central bank will supply its own money in unlimited amounts in exchange for the currency under pressure. Such a solemn declaration, if credible, will deter speculators, because central banks can create unlimited amounts of their own currency to be sold in support of another currency. Once this is known

---

[7] The decision about the conversion rates will be taken at the start of Stage 3. It is therefore conceivable that a country will change its exchange rate after admission (early 1998) but before January 1, 1999. It will then face the almost certain reversal of that exchange-rate manipulation on January 1, 1999.

and accepted by speculators, they will not find it worthwhile to undertake a speculative attack.

If the countries accepted into EMU fail to set up such a commitment technology, they will take a risk. In that case, it will be necessary to allow for a sufficient amount of exchange-rate flexibility. Accordingly, the 15 percent fluctuation margin should be maintained so as to absorb any speculative shocks that may arise. This margin should suffice to weather speculative crises. The authorities may strengthen the exchange-rate system by declaring that the central rates will be the conversion rates. Even if speculators do not fully believe this, they will know that large deviations of the exchange rates from the central rates can involve them in large losses.

Irrevocably Fixed Exchange Rates and Speculation

From January 1, 1999, exchange rates among the participating currencies will be irrevocably fixed. During the following three years, however, these currencies will continue to circulate. They need not be replaced by the euro until 2002.

When this additional stage in the transition process was initially proposed, it met with considerable skepticism from many observers, primarily because of past experience with fixed exchange rates. Sooner or later, fixed exchange rates come under pressure. According to the skeptics, therefore, this additional transition stage is superfluous and will only create more problems on the road to full monetary union.

The European authorities defend the additional period on technical grounds; they regard it as necessary to prepare for the final shift to the single currency. If their interpretation is correct, the additional stage may not lead to speculative crises. The reason is that the ECB will take over monetary policies from the national central banks on January 1, 1999, and it will be able to cope with large changes in the demand for national currencies. Suppose, for example, that large numbers of French residents wish to convert their holdings of francs into deutsche marks between 1999 and 2002. The ECB will supply the additional deutsche marks and retire the francs. It can do this, moreover, until the last francs have disappeared from circulation; the mere substitution of deutsche marks for francs will not jeopardize the systemwide money-supply target that the ECB is likely to pursue.

There may be another reason, however, why this additional stage was added, which relates to Germany's desire to maintain its valuable option to postpone the start of EMU. If this is indeed the case, the stability of the transitional stage is not at all assured, for the market may come to expect that Germany will insist on postponement, and any such expectation may lead to considerable market turbulence. As is well known, the German Constitutional Court has ruled that Germany is entitled to pull out of EMU if EMU does not provide price stability. Such a pullout would still be possible at minimal cost during the transitional stage. To avoid the instability of this low-cost exit option, a strong commitment by Germany will be necessary at the start of 1999. It must declare that it is irrevocably engaged in the process of monetary unification. Otherwise, the Constitutional Court's ruling will hang like a Damocles' sword over the monetary union.

THE APPROACH TO EMU

Charles A.E. Goodhart

1 The Fiscal Question

The program set out in the Maastricht Treaty for reaching monetary union by January 1, 1999, is now looking very tight. The recent cessation of growth in much of Europe has caused the fiscal position in many of the major countries, including France, Germany, and the United Kingdom, to deteriorate relative to prior expectations. Few countries, perhaps only Denmark, Finland, Ireland, and Luxembourg, have achieved the Maastricht limit of 3 percent for budget deficits. The timetable, moreover, is becoming uncomfortably short. It was agreed at the Madrid Summit that the decision about which countries might participate at the start of Stage 3 would be made on the basis of 1997 data as soon as these become reliably available. These data are expected in March 1998.

There appear to be three courses of action available to the European countries that might reasonably expect to join the monetary union at the outset. The first would be to lengthen the timetable by stopping the clock, perhaps by using the clause in Article 109j(4), which can be construed as allowing the European Union (EU) to agree before the end of 1997 to postpone the start date for Stage 3 beyond January 1, 1999. The legality of this course remains uncertain, and there remains much opposition to it, however, particularly within the European Commission, where it is strongly opposed by President Santer. Commission members fear that any flexibility in the agreed upon start date could cause the start to be continuously deferred, especially by a reluctant German public. An initial delay, therefore, might seriously damage the credibility of the economic and monetary union (EMU) itself.

A second option would be to interpret the fiscal criteria gently, for both the deficit and the debt ratio, by giving a loose interpretation to the qualifying clauses in Article 104c(2). The German political elite, however, has expressed its firm opposition to this course, and, given the state of public disenchantment with EMU inside Germany, would find it difficult now to change direction. Indeed, any significant weakening in the application of the criteria might cause Germany to revoke its agreement to join—through an application to the Constitutional Court, for example, through a vote in the Bundesrat, or even as a consequence of the upcoming election in the autumn of 1998.

A third possible option would be to make either additional fiscal cuts in expenditures or increases in taxes. Such measures would be partly offset, however, by their additional deflationary impact on the economy and, hence, on tax revenues. What is more immediately of concern is how fired up public opposition to EMU would be by steps imposed in order to adhere to the fiscal criteria, the rationale for which is highly contentious. It is unfortunate that the final path to EMU is coinciding with a phase of low growth and high unemployment in Europe. This not only makes cyclically inappropriate the timing of the fiscal cuts— although not necessarily their extent—it also means that the EMU process itself may be blamed by the public for the continuation of low growth and high unemployment.

It may well be the case that, with a worsening demographic trend, most European countries should be aiming now for a fiscal surplus over the cycle. But whether or not the Maastricht fiscal criteria happen to be consistent with sound fiscal economics (based, for example, on an estimate of long-term public-expenditure needs to be financed by constant expected tax rates), the criteria were not originally designed or justified on such a basis. As far as one can tell, they were put in place mainly to prevent a member state from choosing to behave imprudently, to prevent it from taking advantage of the comparatively low interest rates offered on government euro-borrowing to build up such a large debt that the European Central Bank (ECB) might suddenly be faced with a choice between an inflationary bailout and a, barely thinkable, decision to let a member state go bankrupt.

The central-bank governors, whose prior work on the Delors Committee and in their own subsequent planning committee largely laid the foundations for Maastricht, have been somewhat inconsistent on this issue. Wearing their hats as Basle Committee supervisors, they proclaimed that OECD government debt should bear a zero credit-risk weighting, but wearing their Delors Committee hats, they constructed an EMU system in which the default risk on member states' government bonds could become significant.[1] But if such default or credit risk on member

---

[1] As the 1995–96 U.S. budgetary battles should remind us, default risk is present even in the strongest countries. Even before EMU, however, central-bank governors were reluctant, no doubt for political reasons, to put themselves in a position of having to allocate any risk-weighting to government debt.

governments' bonds had been, or still could be, properly factored into the various capital-adequacy directives, banks and other financial institutions could not hold large amounts of any government's bonds without holding increasing capital reserves against them. As Graham Bishop (1991, 1992) has rightly argued, the financial system could thereby be given at least partial protection against a default, reducing the need for the authorities to limit fiscal choice for monetary reasons.

One of the adverse side effects of the deficit criterion is that it may reduce the flexibility with which fiscal policy may be used by individual member states to offset adverse shocks, just at the moment when monetary policy may no longer be used for this purpose. In this respect, German minister Theo Waigel's proposed stability pact, whereby member states would aim at a lower deficit in normal times in order to allow some room for the automatic stabilizers to work during cyclical downturns, makes good sense. But there has been, as far as I know, no published justification for proposing that a 1 percent deficit should be the "normal" target level, with 3 percent being the maximum permitted deficit. It could well be that governments should aim for a fiscal *surplus*, on average, in order to allow sufficient room for some fiscal stabilization, both automatic and discretionary, during severe downturns. But perhaps Waigel did not want to frighten the troops.

Waigel did, however, cause a tremor or two by suggesting that any government surpassing the 3 percent limit for more than one year should be required to pay over to the EU budget a fine representing some significant fraction of the assessed overrun. This proposal creates all kinds of difficulties. It would immediately add to the fiscal deficit it is meant to prevent; it would encourage accounting stratagems to reduce the estimated fine; and worst of all, it would inevitably have the effect of raising anti-European venom among the public. Would national parliaments willingly vote for such a tax, and what would happen if they refused? What is needed, instead, is some sanction that would hit the political elite in an offending country *without* impinging on the general public.

2   The Exchange-Rate Question

Membership in the Exchange-Rate Mechanism (ERM) as a Convergence Criterion

Uncertainties about the interpretation of the convergence criteria extend beyond the fiscal criteria to the exchange-rate criterion as well.

This is set out in Article 109j and states that each member state shall fulfill "the observance of the normal fluctuation margins provided for by the exchange rate mechanism of the European Monetary System [EMS], for at least two years, without devaluing against the currency of any other Member State."

The retreat to wider 15 percent bands in August 1993 has clouded the meaning of the term "normal fluctuation" margins. Both the European Monetary Institute (EMI) and the Commission have flinched from any attempt at specific quantification. But what is surely clear is that a member state will have to have been a member of the ERM for the years 1996 and 1997 in order to meet the above wording. Because the United Kingdom is not now a member of the ERM and does not intend to become one in the foreseeable future, it cannot qualify for EMU at the beginning. I have been surprised by comments in the British press that the United Kingdom may be one of the few countries meeting all the criteria at the outset, even if it should choose to avail itself of the opt-out it obtained at Maastricht. I was even more surprised to read a report in the *Financial Times* (Barber, 1995) that Prime Minister Major was of the same view, that prior ERM membership was no longer a prerequisite for entry, and even that the Commission had recoiled from confirming what seems to be patently obvious. The EMI (1995b, p. x) raised such reluctance to an art form in its statement that "under current circumstances, it is not advisable to give a precise operational content to the Treaty provisions regarding exchange rates which could be mechanically applied also to forthcoming periods."[2]

The press reports on the Verona meeting of the ECOFIN Council on April 13 and 14, 1996, suggested that this issue has been clarified. Apparently, the Commission, supported by France, Germany, and Benelux, will require prior membership within the broad-band ERM in order to satisfy the exchange-rate criterion. In view of the possible

[2] Later in the same document (p. 33, box 4.1), the EMI confirms that "the requirement to be a member of the ERM remains an element of the Treaty." At the Royal Institute of International Affairs Conference on EMU in London on March 13 and 14, Klaus Regling of the German Ministry of Finance, Governor Jean Claude Trichet of the Banque de France, Governor Eddie George of the Bank of England, and Sir Leon Brittan, one of the two EC commissioners from the United Kingdom, were all specifically asked for their interpretation of this criterion. Regling said that the Treaty was "clear"; Trichet, that he was consulting his lawyers; and George, that he hoped that the substance of exchange-rate stability, not the formalities of ERM membership, would be the basis for the decision on this issue. Sir Leon waxed eloquent that, should the United Kingdom be otherwise able and willing to join, this problem would "melt away like snow before the Spring sun."

prior uncertainty about the interpretation of this clause, however, those countries not now participating in the ERM (Italy, Sweden, and the United Kingdom) will be allowed until the end of 1996 to rejoin and could still be adjudged to have met that aspect of the criterion. The two-year requirement has, in effect, been shortened to fifteen months, although with casuistry one might argue that by joining in 1996 and being judged in 1998, the two-year requirement minimally remains. For as long as the present Conservative government remains in office, the United Kingdom will not rejoin; how a Labour government might respond is still uncertain.

Several academic colleagues on the Continent take the view that the exchange-rate criterion should be used, if still possible, to exclude the United Kingdom from initial membership, even it wants to join and is, in other respects, entitled to do so. Their point is that membership in EMU is not widely popular either among the British public or among Conservative politicians. The worst scenario for the viability of EMU would be to have one British (Labour) government take the United Kingdom into EMU, only to have a subsequent Conservative government, elected, say in the midst of a severe slump, take the United Kingdom out again. It is thus arguable that profederalists in the United Kingdom and abroad, as well as skeptics, should favor a pre-entry referendum, precisely to defend against the disastrous possibility of the United Kingdom's wounding EMU by revoking the supposedly irrevocable.

I have argued elsewhere (Goodhart, 1996) that EMU cannot be immune to widespread public and political dissatisfaction in any major country, even after the euro has replaced the participants' national currencies, despite empty rhetoric to the contrary. Perhaps the ERM membership issue could be used by Continental politicians as a way of requiring that the United Kingdom hold a referendum before it is allowed to opt in—although it might be difficult for politicians on the Continent to make a proposal that could be construed as interfering in the United Kingdom's internal political processes.

How Should Exchange Rates Be Fixed among the "Ins"?

I turn next, in the context of considering exchange-rate issues, to the question of the "Ins" and the "Outs." Let me first discuss briefly what may happen to the exchange rates of the countries that join EMU at the outset. These insiders face a serious, although somewhat technical, problem. Their exchange rates must be irrevocably fixed on the starting date of January 1, 1999. Their exchange rates may vary against each other, however, and their central rates may be revised between the moment of their selection as Ins and the starting date for Stage 3 (to establish a more user-friendly set of cross-rates against the euro, for example). If such exchange-rate revisions are left until the very last moment, however, say in December 1998, private-sector agents will surely try to anticipate any final alignments, and this could generate massive speculative capital flows in response to rumors or to new information. It is unlikely that official discussions on such a sensitive topic could be kept secret for long, and any leak could lead to most disorderly market conditions.[3]

One alternative that has been canvassed would be to fix at the same moment, say in March 1998, both the identity of the initial participants and the exchange rates that will be adopted among them. It is unlikely, however, that the time and energy available for those decisions would suffice to allow both complex sets of questions to be resolved simultaneously. More important, the institutional arrangements whereby the exchange rates would become irrevocably fixed on January 1, 1999, would not yet be firmly in place. The ECB would not exist, and national central banks would not yet be required, or necessarily willing, to accept at par and without limit the currencies of other participating member states. So long as the national monetary authorities are still independently responsible for setting interest rates in their own money markets, as is supposed to be the case until January 1, 1999, exchange rates can and will diverge from their proclaimed final alignment. Will that matter? If the divergence from the announced final values becomes at all large, it might throw some doubt on the credibility of these future rates. My own view, however, is that the ECB, together with the national central banks of the participating countries, will have the technical ability and market power to prevent large exchange-rate movements, so long as they have the essential political and public support for that exercise. I would therefore expect any interim speculation to be stabilizing, in the sense that it will drive the exchange rates of the participating member states toward their final announced values, unless policies adopted in the meantime by the participating countries are patently inconsistent with the achievement of EMU.

[3] The exercise of setting exchange rates for the Ins may be further complicated, moreover, depending on the interpretation to be given to the Treaty's requirement that the irrevocable fixing "shall not by itself modify the external value of the ECU." Given that only a subset of the EU countries whose currencies are now part of the ECU will join EMU initially, and that some of the Outs may have to devalue at that time, the meaning of this requirement has become opaque, but it might further hinder any planned final parity readjustments. I am grateful to John Arrowsmith for reminding me of this problem.

Other alternatives have been proposed. The Executive Board of the ECB has to be established immediately after the last possible date on which eligible countries are to be chosen, that is by July 1, 1998. Decisions on the selection and introduction of the irrevocably fixed exchange rates may then be delegated to the Governing Council and Executive Board of the ECB as one of its first main tasks.

Another rather neat idea, which has now been widely canvassed, is that the final exchange rates should be established as the average rates ruling over, say, the three years before January 1, 1999. This would give the market a degree of certainty from the outset, while allowing some flexibility in the run-up to January 1. As that final date comes closer, the ultimate value will become ever more firmly established; this should again lead to stabilizing speculation.

The disadvantage of this last solution is that the final exchange rates would result from market happenstance rather than any conscious choice. In particular, market outcomes would not result, except by pure chance, in user-friendly sets of cross-rates (for example, with the euro), but in horrible fractions instead, to seven or so decimal places. Because the key to the whole exercise will be its public acceptability, the choice of user-friendly rates strikes me as important. I would consequently argue for the earliest possible announcement of the final rates, preferably involving a realignment to a user-friendly set of cross-rates. Speculation could then be expected to force actual spot exchange rates toward the final announced values, subject to any remaining interest differentials.

Some, however, fear that any attempt to agree on a final realignment among the insiders would open up a Pandora's box, whereby each nation would seek to achieve a more competitive exchange rate. Whether the final group of insider countries can achieve a set of user-friendly cross-rates without any of them having to undergo a major parity adjustment will remain uncertain until we know the identity of these core countries and can do the accompanying exercise. Experience suggests that it is rarely easy to produce round conversion factors by "small" realignments, even with only a few currencies. If there are, for example, two or more ways of achieving a set of user-friendly rates, with differing implications for real exchange rates, there may be dissension and political deadlock over which to choose.

The case for using averages of market rates as the basis for fixing the exchange rates of participants is the fear that each country will seek its own competitive advantage through a final devaluation and that the participants may become paralyzed and unable to choose any parity realignment. My own view is that this fear is exaggerated. With the participating countries embarking on what will be seen and treated as the start of a grand European design, it seems unlikely that they will risk getting it under way in a fractious spirit by seeking to maximize narrow national advantage. It is, however, not impossible.

Relations between the Ins and Outs

Concerns about "competitive devaluation" have already played a large, although exaggerated, role in discussions about exchange-rate relations between the Ins and Outs. "Competitive devaluation" is to EMU what "fundamental disequilibrium" was to Bretton Woods—a central concept the meaning of which is somewhat difficult to define. In one sense, of course, any devaluation must improve the competitive position of a country, but the countries left outside EMU can hardly be expected to maintain completely fixed exchange rates against the euro, especially when they have just been publicly designated as too weak, too inflationary, and too fiscally profligate to join the union. Indeed, the very fact of being ruled "out" might spark off a speculative attack.

What is becoming clearer is that the positions and objectives of the Outs will be varied. Rather than having a common purpose, the Outs might each seek to engage in bilateral negotiations with the core group of Ins. There may be at least three positions taken by the various Outs. Some—Austria, Belgium, Denmark, and, perhaps, Finland—might wish to mimic as closely as possible the exchange-rate conditions that would have pertained had they been participating in EMU. They could do this by tying their own currencies rigidly to the euro through a currency-board system. The question then would be whether they would have to do so absolutely on their own, relying purely on their own reserves of euros and other foreign-exchange reserves to see themselves through external speculative attacks or internal financial crises, or whether they could expect assistance from the Ins. Unlimited assistance from the Ins must surely be ruled out, because such aid would be tantamount to contradicting the decision to keep these countries out in the first place. But absolute refusal of any assistance would be niggardly and hardly *communautaire*. As in other areas of central banking, constructive ambiguity on a case-by-case basis may be necessary.

At the other extreme are countries that may be unable or unwilling to enter into a standard ERM relationship with the EMU countries. This group might comprise Greece, Italy, and the United Kingdom. Such countries would presumably continue to let their currencies float.

I would presume that the EU institutions, the Council of Ministers and the European Commission, would press these countries to establish some nominal anchor or objective; this could be either an inflation or nominal-income target or an intermediate monetary target.[4] In this case, a competitive devaluation would presumably be defined as a devaluation accompanying a clear failure to abide by the country's chosen nominal anchor. The European bodies would presumably invoke Article 109m of the Maastricht Treaty to give them the standing to express an opinion on the suitability and quantification of the nominal target chosen in each case.

A third group of countries would presumably seek to establish a pegged-but-adjustable exchange-rate relationship with the EMU countries. Niels Thygesen (1996) has argued that the disparity in size and weight between the core Ins and the peripheral Outs, and the absolute priority to be given by the ECB to achieving price stability among the Ins, would probably rule out a simple continuation of the existing EMS. Instead of adopting a grid of bilateral parities, these countries would peg directly to the euro; what the prospective exchange-rate margins would be and what assistance, if any, would be available from the core Ins would have to be determined. The Iberian and Nordic countries might be in this group, but there would be a serious initial problem for them. As already noted, they would have just been publicly designated as weak. The ECB might be too preoccupied with achieving anti-inflationary credibility to offer much, if any, assistance to them on the exchange market, and the EU authorities might attempt to seize this occasion to reestablish narrow margins. If so, the peripheral Outs adopting such pegged exchange rates would be especially vulnerable to speculative attacks at the outset. If then overwhelmed, they might find that a small devaluation might not be credible, whereas a large one might be regarded as "competitive" and hence unacceptable. They would presumably then be forced to let their currencies float.

Only in the case of a chosen preemptive parity adjustment can one make much sense of the term "competitive devaluation." In this instance, one might define it as a devaluation that establishes a more competitive real exchange rate than the rate that existed on some base date, although the difficulties of agreeing to an appropriate base date and of adjusting from a nominal to a comparable real basis are only too obvious.

---

[4] A recent paper by Persson and Tabellini (1996) argues that an inflation target would be more advantageous for the outsider countries than would an exchange-rate peg to the euro.

The more one looks at the term "competitive devaluation," the more slippery and difficult it becomes. A nominal devaluation that is accompanied by an expansionary monetary policy, for example, is unlikely to make the devaluing country excessively competitive for long, because the resulting faster-climbing domestic inflation is likely to bring the real exchange rate back to its predevaluation level rather quickly. Yet a nominal devaluation that is not accompanied by a more expansionary monetary policy is unlikely to reflect a conscious attempt to gain a trading advantage but, as with Italy's recent experience, may be forced by speculative attacks based on political or other noneconomic concerns. It takes a rare combination of circumstances to achieve a purposeful, consciously chosen, devaluation that succeeds in achieving any long-lasting competitive advantage by altering the real exchange rate. Politicians, officials, and economists who are most concerned about this supposed problem should be required to state exactly how a "competitive devaluation" should be defined.

LINKING THE INS AND OUTS

Daniel Gros

Only a few of the fifteen member states of the European Union (EU) will participate at the start of Stage 3 of economic and monetary union (EMU), scheduled to begin on January 1, 1999. On present performance, only three to five countries around France and Germany are likely to be part of this avant-garde.[1] This raises the question of how the exchange-rate relations between the Ins and the Outs should be organized.

There is a strictly legal aspect to this issue in that one of the convergence criteria in the Maastricht Treaty (Article 109j[1]) is "the observance of the normal fluctuation margins provided for by the exchange rate mechanism [ERM] of the European Monetary System [EMS], for at least two years, without devaluing against the currency of any other member state." The Treaty states, in addition, that once EMU has started, there must be, at least every two years, an examination of the countries that have not yet qualified to enter the monetary union. Such a country may join EMU only if it fulfills the convergence criteria. The Treaty thus implicitly assumes that the exchange-rate mechanism of the EMS will continue to exist. This does not necessarily imply that the EMS must continue in exactly its present form. Because the circumstances will change radically once Stage 3 begins, one might even argue that the EMS must change. It is clear, however, that formal participation in a reformed exchange-rate mechanism (as opposed to mere stability of the exchange rate independently of any such mechanism) will be one of the requirements for entry after 1999. The ECOFIN Council at Verona confirmed this interpretation of the Treaty in April 1996.[2] It is thus clear that some form of exchange-rate mechanism will have to be created and that all countries that want to participate eventually in EMU will have to be part of it.

1 A New Exchange-Rate Mechanism?

The Treaty mandates only that there has to be some kind of exchange-rate mechanism. The interesting question from an economic point of

---

[1] The term "avant-garde" is meant to suggest that the starting group does not form an exclusive "core," but that it will be joined quickly by most of the other EU countries.

[2] ECOFIN denotes the Council of Ministers when it includes the ministers of economics and finance.

view is what form that mechanism should take. Some observers have argued that common inflation targets would be preferable to an exchange-rate target (Dewatripont et al., 1995; Persson and Tabellini, 1996; Spaventa, 1996a). The present paper assumes that the conditions under which inflation targets are desirable, namely, unstable money demand in the euro area and few shocks to exchange rates, are not likely to prevail. The choice between inflation and exchange-rate targets is really more apparent than real, because the Treaty also imposes an inflation target in the form of the convergence requirement on inflation (which must not be more than 1.5 percent above that of the three best performers).

The function of a new exchange-rate mechanism, already known as "EMS 2," for the countries that do not participate immediately in EMU would be to limit short-run exchange-rate variability and avoid misalignments. The experience of 1993 has shown that even countries such as France, which has strong fundamentals, may come under pressure, and the near crisis of 1995 shows that political uncertainty may set in motion a self-validating chain of higher interest rates that lead to higher budget deficits and, in turn, to higher interest rates. For a formal description of this kind of speculative attack, see Gros (1995b).

An exchange-rate mechanism would thus be not only legally required but also potentially useful in limiting exchange-rate variability and misalignments of the currencies outside EMU. The form it should take and its feasibility in 1999 cannot be predicted at this time, because its nature will depend on the number of countries that remain outside EMU initially and the prospects of their joining soon. Consider the following two extreme scenarios:

(1) By early 1998, eleven countries have made enough progress to participate in EMU, and the United Kingdom elects to "opt in." Only Greece, Italy, Portugal, and Sweden still have excessive budget deficits, but the last three of these have made so much progress in fiscal consolidation and in reducing inflation that they will probably be able to join a year or two later.

(2) Only France, Germany, and a few small countries participate in 1999. The United Kingdom has confirmed its intention to opt out, and convergence in the rest of the European Union has been very slow, so that the other countries will need some years before they can join EMU.

It is apparent that the nature of the exchange-rate system that will be needed, the EMS 2, will be radically different depending on which of these two scenarios most closely describes the outcome. Under the first scenario, there is no need for a full-fledged exchange-rate system, because exchange rates are likely to be stable anyway. Under the second, by contrast, there would be a real need for a system to limit exchange-rate fluctuations.

Although one cannot know in mid-1996 how many countries will join EMU in 1999 (the Ins) and how much convergence those remaining outside (the Outs) will have achieved, a few simple considerations show that it will not be possible under any circumstance to recreate the old EMS. The main constraint is the difference in size between the Ins taken collectively and the Outs taken individually. This has two implications: asymmetry and bilateralism—or "hub and spoke."

Asymmetry

Even if the avant-garde contains only France, Germany, and a few smaller countries, it will be several times as large in terms of GDP and trade as the set of countries that remain outside EMU (excluding the United Kingdom). The difference will be even larger in terms of the sizes of financial markets and reputations for stability. A formally symmetric system like the EMS becomes impossible under these circumstances. Even in the old ERM, Germany played a central role, although, in terms of trade and GDP, it never accounted for more than 45 percent of the area covered.

Hub and Spokes

The trade of the periphery with the core that will represent the "hub" of the system is several times larger than the trade among the "spokes" (the likely outsiders). The new system will thus not be multilateral. It will be effectively bilateral, in that it regulates the bilateral relations between the euro and the outsiders' currencies.

Figure 1 illustrates these facts by grouping the main participants in the post-EMU environment into four boxes proportionate in size to each group's GDP. The figure thus shows the relative sizes of the Ins and Outs and the strength of trade links between them. It is apparent that the avant-garde block is much larger than that of the Outs, which has been split into two subgroups: the "willing outsiders" and the United Kingdom and Denmark.

For the avant-garde, trade with the rest of the world is much more important than trade with either the willing outsiders or the United Kingdom and Denmark. The behavior of the dollar and yen exchange rates are thus more important than the behavior of the exchange rates

FIGURE 1

INS AND OUTS: RELATIVE SIZES AND TRADE LINKS

(*in billions of ECUs*)

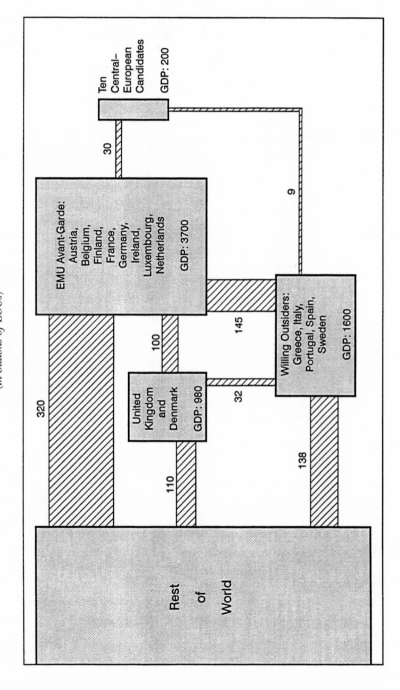

of the Outs. The European Central Bank (ECB) will therefore be much more inclined to react to developments affecting the value of the euro against the dollar than to be concerned about possible competitive devaluations by the outsiders.

For the willing outsiders, the situation is different: Their exchange-rate policies are likely to be focused on the euro, not only because they hope to participate in EMU, but also because most of their trade is with EMU. For the United Kingdom and Denmark, the relative strength of the trade links is inverted: the rest of the world will be more important than EMU as long as EMU comprises only the avant-garde. Once the willing outsiders have joined EMU, the situation will change, because at that point, trade with the rest of the world (110 billion ECUs) will be smaller than trade with a large EMU (132 billion ECUs).

Finally, there is no economic rational for a coalition of the willing outsiders with the United Kingdom. Their trade links are not important. It is also interesting to note that the ten candidate countries in Central Europe ("future willings") are economic dwarfs. Most of their trade, moreover, is with the EMU avant-garde; their links with the Outs are insignificant.

All willing outsiders have been lumped together in one rectangle in Figure 1. In reality, however, they differ enormously from each other in terms of their trade links and convergence efforts. This does not imply that each outsider should have a different exchange-rate arrangement. On the contrary, for legal reasons, the same type of arrangement has to be offered to all outsiders. Even if all outsiders are willing to enter the same system, however, it will not actually work in the same way for each participant.

The case of the United Kingdom will present a particular problem if the British government decides to opt out in 1998 and confirms its refusal to enter into an agreement concerning the exchange rate of the pound. There is little one can do if the U.K. government insists on this position. The other member countries will probably cooperate with the ECB, however, to create a system that stabilizes exchange rates. I have indicated why I believe it is too early to discuss the details of such a system, but two features should be part of any system that is finally adopted. First, support from the ECB in terms of intervention obligations should be linked to the convergence efforts of the outsiders. The closer a country gets to satisfying the criteria for full EMU membership, the more support it should receive from the ECB in defending its exchange rate if it comes under a speculative attack. Second, there must be a limit to the obligations of the ECB. The ECB cannot underwrite a system that forces it to intervene in unlimited amounts at some prespecified exchange rate. That would jeopardize its primary responsibility, which is to maintain price stability for its members.

Although the precise form of an EMS 2 will presumably be known before 1999, its actual functioning after 1999 will depend much more on the relative sizes of its members (mentioned above) and the degree of convergence achieved by the outsiders at that date than on the formal rules of the game.

It is often argued that the countries that remain outside will be tempted to resort to competitive devaluations. But this fear, which is based on recent experience, seems to be unfounded. Exchange rates are difficult to control, because they evolve with market expectations about future policy. It will therefore be difficult for any government (or national central bank) to "engineer" a competitive depreciation without starting a cycle of inflationary expectations and rising interest rates that will be difficult to control. Moreover, the convergence criterion on exchange-rate stability will continue to apply after 1999, and any country that is tempted to pursue a "beggar-thy-neighbor" exchange-rate policy will pay the price of a further delay in gaining EMU membership.

How tight the exchange-rate system will be after EMU has started depends essentially on the Outs, but that is not likely to be the key political problem in early 1998. The chief political problem will be posed by the "near Ins," that is, the countries that just fail to satisfy one or more of the convergence criteria. These countries will argue that EMU should be delayed because they will suffer from speculative attacks and higher interest rates if they are excluded. They might even claim that a "vital national interest" is at stake and might exert political pressure to delay the start of EMU. This would be difficult from a legal point of view, because the Maastricht Treaty says that those that do not want to participate, or cannot participate, will respect the will of the others to go ahead. In 1998, moreover, the European Council will not need to take a vote on the start of EMU, because EMU will start in principle automatically on January 1, 1999. In the life of the European Union, however, politics is often more important than the legal details of the Treaty. If some of the near Ins want to delay EMU, they might argue that the fiscal criteria have not been objectively applied, or they might withhold their cooperation on other important issues (for example, the Intergovernmental Conference on Political Union). It is therefore critical to take the interests of these countries into account. A postponement to allow the near Ins to catch up is not desirable, because there will always be some country that is close to fulfilling all the criteria. How should one deal with this problem?

2 A Concrete Proposal

The countries that are excluded from the start of EMU, despite being very close, need some reassurance from the European Union that an EMU comprising only the avant-garde is only a temporary phenomenon and that the others can be sure of joining once they have converged. This is certainly the intention of the Treaty, but what if initial exclusion makes convergence much more difficult, even with the aid of a new EMS?

The best solution would be to grant a form of *associate* status in EMU. An almost convergent country could be invited to come under the EMU umbrella to benefit from lower interest rates, but it would not participate in the management of the common monetary policy until it had converged in fiscal terms. This arrangement could be achieved technically by a unilateral declaration that the country concerned accept all the obligations arising from membership in EMU.[3] It would be preferable, however, to have *a formal agreement* between the European Union (or, rather, the ECB) and the country concerned, and political support from the Council of Ministers, because this would make the arrangement much more credible in the markets. The agreement would mainly specify that the national currency would be irrevocably linked to the euro without margins and that the national central bank would follow the monetary policy of the ECB as if it were a full member of EMU.

In essence, the country would give up its national monetary policy and replace it with that of the ECB—just as full participants would do—but it would play no role in the making of ECB policy. More precisely, its exchange rate would be irrevocably fixed, its payments

[3] The government would have to declare its acceptance of the obligations arising from Articles 104c(9) and (11) on the excessive deficits procedure; Articles 105(1), (2), (3), and (5), on monetary policy; 105a on notes and coins; and 108a on empowering the ESCB. The national central bank would also have to accept the obligations resulting from the ESCB Statute (Articles 3, 9, 12.1, 14.3, 16, 18, 19, 20, 22, 23, 30–34, and 52). The restrictions specified in paragraphs 3 to 6 of Article 43 of the Statute, however, would apply. In addition, the country concerned would not participate in decisions under Articles 109, on exchange-rate relations with the rest of the world, and 109a(2)(b), on membership of the Executive Board of the ESCB.

systems would be unified with that of the monetary union, and it would be directly affected by actions of the ECB. It's national central bank would have to implement the decisions of the ECB and to transfer a portion of its foreign-exchange reserves to the ESCB. The country would, moreover, be subject to the full excessive deficit procedure, including the provisions pertaining to sanctions.

All this would be officially acknowledged by the European Union in conjunction with a convergence program outlining the way in which the country would, with the help of lower interest rates, satisfy the fiscal criterion by a certain deadline, for example, within one or two years. Acknowledgment by both the European Union and the ECB should make this arrangement credible and ensure that market interest rates in the country converge quickly to the level of the avant-garde. It may be noted that the country's actual debt-service burden would decline only gradually, however, until retirement of the outstanding high-interest debt. Depending on the maturity structure, this might take two years.

Associate status in EMU can deliver benefits in terms of lower interest rates only if it is credible. Credibility can be provided by the endorsement of the ECB, but it would be immensely strengthened if markets are convinced that the country's exchange rate can be defended under any circumstance. This should be the case if the proposed arrangement is seen to be a "currency board." A currency board is credible if the national central bank possesses adequate foreign reserves to guarantee the convertibility of all of its liabilities (the monetary base), in this instance, convertibility into euros. Would this be the case? Gros (1996) shows that most of the central banks that might be candidates for associate status do, indeed, have sufficient reserves to make the currency-board strategy credible.

All the candidates for associate membership in EMU could thus be confident of operating a tight link with the core group even under a worst-case scenario. If the markets know that there is no chance of forcing a break in the link to the euro, they will regard it as credible. Any country that chooses this method could increase credibility by passing a law requiring its national central bank to defend the exchange rate with unsterilized interventions. In the event of a totally unjustified speculative attack, moreover, the ECB would be likely to help the country concerned. If the country's underlying fundamentals are sound, therefore, credibility should not be a problem. If the fundamentals are not sound, the ECB would not recommend this currency-based approach, and no country would (or should) dare to try it against ECB advice.

Technical viability is, of course, only a necessary, and not a sufficient, condition for the stability of a currency-board arrangement. The reason why central banks usually sterilize their interventions is that the large increases in interest rates that might otherwise result are potentially unacceptable, because of their macroeconomic consequences (the United Kingdom in 1992, for example), because they could endanger the stability of the banking system (Sweden in 1992), or because of their fiscal implications (Belgium in 1993 and Italy in 1992 and 1995).

The associate members of EMU would be in a better position than Sweden or the United Kingdom because their banking systems would already operate in euros. A speculative attack would not endanger the euro's stability. They can also make sure their position will be stronger than the positions of Belgium or Italy if they offer to convert all outstanding public debt into euros. Once this has happened (most bond holders will be happy to get euro bonds), movements in domestic interest rates that could be caused by a speculative attack would no longer have any implications for public finances.

Associate membership in EMU will not be a magic wand that eliminates all problems. It represents an option, however, for countries that are very close to qualifying for full membership. Irrevocably fixing the exchange rate, with the prospect of full participation in EMU after a couple of years, is fundamentally different from the fixing of exchange rates in the environment of the 1980s, when exchange rates were high and variable, or during the early 1990s, when some currencies were clearly overvalued. The argument that experience has shown that fixing the exchange rate is impossible because financial markets can attack any exchange rate should therefore not be overrated. There will be little reason for financial markets to attack an exchange rate if inflation is low, deficits are close to 3 percent of GDP (possibly even below), debt ratios are declining, the current-account balance indicates a good competitive position, and the public debt is denominated in euros.

Only countries that have done their basic homework should be encouraged to pursue associate membership in EMU. In order to qualify, a country's budget deficit, when calculated at avant-garde interest rates, should fall at least below 3 percent of GDP. This discipline will ensure that the debt ratio will be declining once the lower interest rates take effect. It bears reiterating that the country in question will not participate in the decisionmaking organs of the ESCB, an exclusion that will make it clear that the convergence criteria have not been suspended. The credibility of the ECB will therefore not be diminished.

3 Concluding Remarks

The relation between the Ins and the Outs will be the chief economic and political problem for the European Union once it has become clear that EMU will actually start and that specific countries will participate in the first wave. The Treaty mandates that some sort of exchange-rate mechanism has to exist after 1999. The nature of this mechanism will depend less on the formal rules that are likely to be adopted before the end of 1996 than on the realities of 1999: an avant-garde that is several times larger than the outsiders and the progress in convergence achieved by the willing outsiders. The most likely outcome is a system that operates *de facto* as a unilateral peg, whatever its formal rules. The countries that are very close to satisfying the convergence criteria should thus forego this uncertain lifeline and jump immediately on board EMU as associate members.

COEXISTING WITH THE EURO: PROSPECTS AND RISKS AFTER VERONA

Luigi Spaventa

1 Introduction

The drafters of the Maastricht Treaty's Title VI on "Economic and Monetary Policy" left a particularly complicated puzzle for their successors to solve. If, at the ultimate date set for the beginning of the third stage of economic and monetary union (EMU), only some of the member states of the European Union (EU) fulfill the necessary conditions for the adoption of the euro, and if, as a result, only the currencies of those countries have irrevocably fixed exchange rates, is there to be an exchange-rate arrangement between the euro currency bloc and the remaining EU currencies, and, if so, what kind of arrangement? The Treaty leaves this issue open and provides no guidance for reconciling the contrasting interests of the parties involved. Worse, a number of inconsistencies in the Treaty's provisions raise unnecessary hurdles in the way of a solution.

For over two years after the Maastricht Treaty was ratified by all member states, this issue remained undetected or neglected at the official level, because the crisis of the EMS made the prospect of a single currency increasingly uncertain. Only as the drive to EMU gathered fresh political momentum under the favorable economic conditions of the 1994–95 recovery did the problem become apparent. It is now at the fore of academic debate and of technical and political-economic diplomacy.[1] The conclusions of the presidency of the European Council at Madrid (December 15–16, 1995), having confirmed "unequivocally" that January 1, 1999, will be the starting date for monetary union, stated that "the future relationships between Member

---

This paper is a sequel to, and for some points draws on, an earlier paper by the author (Spaventa, 1996b).

[1] Academics became aware of the problem before diplomats and politicians did. See, among others, Gros and Thygesen (1992), Arrowsmith (1995b, 1996), De Grauwe (1995), Dewatripont et al. (1995), Kenen (1995b, 1995c), Gros (1996), Persson and Tabellini (1996), Spaventa (1996b), Thygesen (1996), and Wyplosz (1996).

50

States participating in the euro area and non-participating Member States will have to be defined prior to [that] move." The Council asked the ECOFIN Council,[2] together with the European Commission and the European Monetary Institute (EMI), to study the problem, and after some work done by the Monetary Committee and the EMI, the (informal) ECOFIN Council, meeting in Verona on April 12, 1996, took a first step in that direction.

The Council decided in principle that there should and will be an exchange-rate arrangement—dubbed "EMS 2"—between the euro area and those EU members remaining outside EMU, and it specified some general features of such an arrangement. Although the Council went further than many expected, the number of unsettled problems is still huge—naturally so, perhaps, in view of the existing economic difficulties, conflicting interests, and institutional constraints.

The discussion that follows examines the puzzle created by both the Treaty provisions and the different motivations of the players and, in order to appraise the choices made in Verona, considers the broad alternatives discussed there. It reviews the many issues yet to be settled and argues that the stability of the system will very much depend on the solution given to the problem of intervention. It assumes that the third and final stage of EMU will start on January 1, 1999, and will not be postponed, and that given the conditions set out in the Treaty, only some member states, and only some of the larger ones, will qualify for immediate admission.

2 The Pieces of the Puzzle

The Treaty

One set of provisions in the Treaty appears to imply that the exchange-rate mechanism (ERM) of the European Monetary System (EMS) will survive after Stage 3 begins if there are member states with a "derogation" (countries that have not qualified) or states such as Denmark and the United Kingdom that have opted out of joining EMU. These provisions state that (1) The derogation of a member state can be abrogated if it is decided—at the state's own request or as a result of periodic (at least every two years) reports by the European Commission and the European Central Bank (ECB), following the procedure laid down in Articles 109k(2) and 109j(1)—that the country fulfills the

---

[2] The Council of Ministers when also attended by the ministers of economics and finance.

necessary conditions for admission, one of which is "the observance of the normal fluctuation margins provided for by the exchange rate mechanism of the European Monetary System, for at least two years, without devaluing against the currency of any other Member State" (Article 109j[1]).

(2) From the beginning of the third stage, a member state with a derogation "shall treat its exchange-rate policy as a matter of common interest" and take account, in so doing," of the experience acquired in cooperation within the framework" of the EMS (Article 109m).

(3) The ECB "shall take over those tasks of the EMI which, because of the derogations of one or more Member States, still have to be performed in the third stage" (Article 44 of the Protocol on the Statute of the ESCB and ECB). The tasks of the EMI include, among others, administering the very short-term financing mechanism provided for by the agreement of March 13, 1979, between the member states' central banks laying down the operating procedures for the EMS; assuming the tasks of the European Monetary Cooperation Fund; and monitoring the working of the EMS (Articles 4.1 and 6.1–3 of the Protocol on the Statute of the EMI).

But although the Treaty issues no explicit death certificate, it is agreed that the EMS, in its present form, will cease to exist as the third stage begins. First, the ECB, as a new subject, is not a party to the 1979 central-bank agreement regarding the procedures for the EMS, and there is no provision making it a successor to the obligations undertaken by the national central banks. Second, when the EMI goes into liquidation upon the establishment of the ECB, the mechanism for the creation of official European currency units (ECUs) shall be unwound. More to the point, the claims and liabilities arising from the very short-term and short-term financing and support mechanisms of the EMS must be settled by the first day of the third stage (Article 23 of the EMI Statute). Finally, a third set of Treaty provisions makes it difficult either to replicate the old EMS in an environment comprising a euro club and a number of outside community currencies or even to replace it with an analogous arrangement. The EMS was based on a resolution of the European Council and, at the Council's request, on a subsequent agreement among central banks in accordance with the rules set forth by the resolution. At first sight, it is difficult to reconcile this procedure with the Treaty. The Council's powers to conclude agreements on an exchange-rate system for the euro are explicitly confined to agreements in relation to "non-Community" currencies (Article 109); the possibility of agreements involving EU currencies is never mentioned. As for the ECB, it shall not "take instructions from Community institutions or bodies" (Article 7 of the ESCB and ECB Statute). At least in principle, therefore, a resolution of the Council instructing the ECB to conclude an exchange-rate agreement linking the euro with other EU currencies would be nonbinding and would not violate the ECB's independence.

Summing up, the Treaty implies the existence of a European exchange-rate arrangement with outsider currencies in the third stage, not only for reasons of substance, but because the observance of normal fluctuation margins around a recognized parity remains a condition for later admission, for which countries with a derogation are entitled to apply. The ERM established in 1979 will cease to exist, but the Treaty is silent on a possible alternative; worse, it makes it formally difficult to establish one.

Motivations and Consensus

Treaties are not cast in bronze. If constitutions can be amended, so can treaties. Alternatively, if the amending process is too cumbersome, shrewd lawyers can justify bending the rules toward a solution that everybody agrees to be sensible and desirable. That is, however, the point. Whether it is a matter of amending or of interpreting, there must be an *ex ante* consensus on the desired outcome. There has been no such consensus in Europe on the shape, or even the desirability, of an exchange-rate arrangement between the euro and the outsider currencies—another reason, perhaps, why the problem has remained hidden for so long. Conflicting interests are apparent not only between the insiders and the outsiders, but also within each group.

The insiders' attitude is somewhat schizophrenic. On the one hand, a firm setting of parities linking the euro with the currencies of the outsiders is deemed indispensable to exorcise the ghost of "competitive devaluations." It is feared that the existence of floating EU currencies outside the euro area might cause an unwarranted real appreciation of the euro, thereby jeopardizing the existence of the Single Market and leading to demands for trade and financial sanctions against the (depreciating) floaters. The monetary authorities of the potential insiders, however, are convinced that exchange-rate agreements with currencies that are weaker by definition—because their countries cannot meet the Treaty's standards of stability—would pollute the purity and endanger the reputation of the newly created ECB and the newly born euro, because the ECB would be burdened by intervention obligations that might interfere with independently set money-supply targets.

53

Potential outsiders are a mixed bunch. An opt-out clause exempts the United Kingdom from the reporting and examination procedure required of other countries before the start of the third phase, unless it decides to seek admission. Even if Britain remains an outsider, it will not bear the stigma of having failed an exam set by its peers—nonentry as a choice, rather than as the undesired result of forced exclusion, will have low costs in terms of credibility and reputation. Offering Britain an exchange-rate agreement with the euro, aimed at later admission, not only offers no particular benefit; it might also be costly. Participation would align Britain with the other outsiders and blur its distinctive status, and nonparticipation might prove to be one opt-out too many in Britain's already complicated relations with the European Union.

For the common outsider—one with a derogation because it cannot comply with the conditions for admission—the political and economic costs of nonentry are very high. Once the final stage of monetary union has begun, and the stronger countries are participating, any further debate about the alleged benefits of the single currency, and even its economic desirability, loses relevance. Although it may still be argued that an individual country might do better without the single currency, it is certain that the mere existence of a single-currency club of nations will make life difficult for those that do not belong. The problem is more one of costs than of benefits. Unless some link is established with the insiders, with a view to subsequent admission, the outsider will experience higher actual and expected exchange-rate volatility, greater exposure and sensitivity of its financial-asset prices to domestic and foreign shocks, and (as a result) higher interest-rate differentials vis-à-vis the euro countries. This will, in turn, impair the prospects of quick convergence to the Maastricht criteria, with further damaging consequences in the financial markets. The Treaty conditions tend to produce multiple equilibria. Without a safety net, the outsiders are at risk of being led toward a "bad" equilibrium when a better one could be achievable. Exclusion is bound to reduce a country's political weight in the European Union (Arrowsmith, 1995b, 1996). If, furthermore, the lack of structured relations with the euro area dims the prospect of admission in the near future, politicians and public opinion may become more reluctant to make the additional effort required to complete convergence. Countries with a derogation thus have an interest in obtaining an exchange-rate arrangement with the euro that is as similar as possible to the arrangement of the old EMS.

3 Alternative Proposals and the Choice at Verona

When the gaps and inconsistencies in the Treaty became apparent once the problem of relations between the euro area and the outsider currencies surfaced at the political level, EU members were faced with a choice between two basic options: to work out an acceptable exchange-rate arrangement or to do without an arrangement altogether, possibly replacing it with another form of policy coordination.[3] Let us consider the merits and drawbacks of these two options.

The British view (now an Anglo-Scandinavian view) has for some time been that the pegging of currencies in a formal exchange-rate arrangement is neither a necessary nor a particularly desirable preliminary step for admission to the monetary union. In addition to its political motivations, this view also rests on arguments of substance. It states, first, that some flexibility of nominal exchange rates may help, rather than hinder, the process of convergence if shocks affect an individual economy, and, second, that experience has shown the extent to which exchange-rate systems based on formal commitments to central parities, whether multilateral or bilateral, have become vulnerable to speculative attacks and to capital movements in general. Interventions are either inane or, if sufficient to stem the tide of capital flows, incompatible with domestic monetary stability. Mandatory and coordinated inflation targeting in the euro area and in the outsider countries may be a better and more effective way than exchange-rate pegging to ensure sufficient exchange-rate stability and to converge to low inflation. Inflation targeting now has powerful theoretical backing, both in general and in the specific context of designing the relations between those inside and outside a monetary union. In this latter context, a model by Persson and Tabellini (1996) suggests that the advantages of a coordinated European system of inflation targets over an EMS-like system are greater symmetry in the face of shocks, added credibility to a low-inflation policy, less exchange-rate volatility, and safeguards against deliberate competitive devaluations.[4] The British option might, in addition, avoid all the complications inherent in setting up a new exchange-rate mechanism adapted to the existence of a euro bloc at the center of the system.

---

[3] Spaventa (1996b) and Thygesen (1996) survey the options available within the economic, political, and institutional constraints.

[4] Dewatripont et al. (1995) provide less formal arguments for coordinated inflation targeting after the start of the third stage.

For a number of reasons, however, and especially if the Treaty provisions are taken as a given, the British option cannot be viewed as a satisfactory solution. First, inflation targeting is a medium-term exercise, often yielding very wide yearly bands. Even granting its alleged benefits, therefore, it is better suited to ensuring the peaceful coexistence of the euro with the currencies of a number of member states ready or willing to accept an outsider status *indefinitely* (as may be the case with the United Kingdom). It is difficult to see how it can be relevant for a state not participating in the monetary union from the start but aiming to fulfill the necessary conditions for admission at an early date. To decide at that early date whether the medium-term target has been met or missed may be premature. More important, one of the conditions to be fulfilled for the adoption of the single currency already sets a precise, although relative, inflation target: "an average rate of inflation, observed over a period of one year before the examination, that does not exceed by more than 1½ percentage points that of, at most, the three best performing Member States" (Article 1 of the Protocol on the Convergence Criteria). The ultimate objective, therefore, has already been stated, and it is up to the national authorities to decide by which means they want to achieve it.

Second, the exchange-rate stabilizing effect of an inflation target is very far from being assured. True, adoption of an inflation target would prevent a country from engaging in competitive devaluations. But is that a problem? Neither the 1992 crisis nor the later depreciation of some currencies thereafter can be construed as competitive devaluations, that is, as cases in which domestic policies were *deliberately* aimed at causing a depreciation of the exchange rate. If anything, monetary and fiscal policies were typically tightened after the crisis. Further devaluations and spates of depreciation of a floating currency such as the lira were most often the result of external and domestic political shocks. Inflation targeting would not by itself eliminate the exchange-rate volatility inflicted by such shocks (of which the Mexican crisis is one example), especially for currencies made intrinsically weaker by the creation of a bloc of strong currencies.[5] Finally, the necessary conditions for the adoption of a single currency listed in the

---

[5] As Borgatta (1936, p. 251) wrote in reviewing the experience of the French franc and Italian lira in the 1920s: "Political incidents at home, monetary and political crises in other countries, insofar as it is believed that they can bring about changes in domestic monetary conditions, may cause a collapse of confidence and episodes of panic which do not occur, or occur to a much more limited extent, in a system of legally stabilized currency."

Treaty include both an inflation condition and an exchange-rate condition. The British position implies that we are simply to neglect the latter when deciding which member states comply with the required criteria: it implies that even in the 1998 examination procedure, participation in the still existing EMS should not be required for admission. But can a specific and very precise Treaty provision be disregarded, even if disregarding it makes good economic sense, without undergoing a process of formal revision? If it can, why disregard only that provision and not others that are no less, and are perhaps more, objectionable? It is only natural that the prevailing political decision should be to leave this Pandora's box unopened.

This is what they decided to do in Verona, where, as a result, the majority opted for attempting to design a new exchange-rate arrangement to succeed the EMS. The objections to the British option cannot hide the well-known difficulties adhering to this alternative, chosen perhaps more from necessity than from conviction. The difficulties are summarized in the oxymoron that was the accepted definition of the EMS: a system of "fixed-but-adjustable" parities. Can such a system be stable and, beyond that, credible? Fundamentals are important, but they do not by themselves ensure credibility when capital movements can be of a size sufficient to fulfill the expectations of a change of parities. Supporting interventions can buttress credibility only if the market perceives them to be potentially unlimited and unconstrained by other considerations. Unlimited support by one central bank to another, however, conflicts with a bank's commitment to domestic price stability, an objective that has higher priority, and the markets know it. Alternatively, the band around the parity may be set so wide as to tolerate large swings of the exchange rate without requiring intervention, as is the case with the enlarged bands surrounding most EMS currencies since 1993. If exchange-rate stability is the result that is sought, however, this can hardly be considered a satisfactory solution.

The 1992 crisis is invoked as conclusive evidence supporting these strictures against any EMS-like system, but the evidence is not wholly convincing. First, it ignores the remarkably long period of tranquillity that the EMS enjoyed until 1991. Second, taking into account the shock of German unification and its effects, the 1992 crisis could more aptly be turned into an argument against the uncritical and rigid acceptance of a strong-currency option that prevented a timely adjustment of parities. Third, fundamentals are much better aligned now than they were in 1992, when weaker countries had overvalued exchange rates and huge domestic imbalances. These have, to a large extent, been corrected.

All this may not be sufficient, however, to allay the misgiving raised by an attempt to resurrect the exchange-rate mechanism, unless the new version is tailored to the needs of the new situation created by the launching of monetary union with only some EU currencies aboard. A mechanism replacing the EMS once the third stage of EMU begins should be conceived, not as a permanent system, but as a bridge to the single currency, at least for most outsider currencies. Each country's prospect for admission, to be judged by its progress in complying with the required conditions, will crucially affect the credibility of the arrangement for that particular country's currency. To serve this bridging purpose, the design of a new EMS should, unlike the old, feature an element of conditionality, based on each outsider's compliance with a convergence program.[6] It should ensure that the deserving are helped fully and with conviction, whereas the laggards are sanctioned by withdrawing support for their currencies. That is all that is necessary to leave the door open to the former, while preserving the necessary flexibility.

It is too early to say whether we are moving in this direction. The broad guidelines for the new exchange-rate arrangement on which the gentlemen of Verona seem to have agreed leave many problems unsolved and may still lead to an unsatisfactory outcome. They have agreed that the new system must be flexible and anchored to the euro, and that the central rates with the euro will be set and, if need be, adjusted by agreement, with fluctuation margins around them. They have, in addition, agreed that some purely fictional elements of the EMS, such as the divergence indicator and the pretence of symmetry, will be explicitly discarded, that only the outsiders will be expected to adjust their policies in the case of tensions, and that although there will be obligatory bilateral interventions at the margin, the ECB can invoke a suspension clause when, in its view, intervention would conflict with the objective of price stability. The ECB will also be given the power to trigger the procedure for a realignment. The new system may be put in place by an agreement between the ECB and the outsiders' central banks. In general, from what is known, it looks as if the ECB has been given the dominant role, at the expense of the ECOFIN Council, the Economic and Financial Committee (which will succeed the Monetary Committee), and the Commission.

---

[6] Conditionality is proposed by Thygesen (1996) and, with more explicit reference to interventions, by Spaventa (1996b) and Wyplosz (1996).

It is now time to consider the main themes that require further work in the near future and to appraise the risks that should be avoided. I shall examine in increasing order of relevance some of the issues still to be settled and the problems that may arise.

4 Conditionality or Discretion? Unsettled Issues and Problems Ahead

Hub and Spokes or a Grid?

In the EMS, a grid of bilateral parities connecting all pairs of currencies was derived from the agreed upon parity of each currency with the ECU, and intervention margins were set for each pair of currencies around these parities. In the new system, with the euro—a currency in its own right—solidly at the center, and with given central parities between the euro and each participating outsider currency, margins may come to be set and interventions triggered only in relation to these bilateral parities. As a result, the permitted margins of fluctuation between two outsider currencies will be wider than those between each currency and the euro. Because this consequence is likely to be of little practical relevance, however, a hub-and-spokes system, which permits greater flexibility in the setting of intervention margins, would be preferable.[7]

Width of Margins

A hub-and-spokes arrangement would be more compatible with bands of different widths than would a bilateral grid. Adequate flexibility can be insured by tailoring conditionality to the situation of each outsider. Allowing different bands for different currencies (up to a pre-set maximum that could coincide with the present 15 percent), according to whether a particular country is more or less near to full compliance with the convergence criteria, would help serve this purpose. In this way, the burden of intervention obligations would be lighter for countries more remote from admission and hence more vulnerable to currency instability. A variety of bands may also be helpful in solving the problem of compulsion with regard to membership in the monetary system.

Membership in the System: Compulsory or Optional?

Should a country seeking later admission to the monetary union become a member of the system that succeeds the EMS? According to the

[7] For this to occur, one outsider currency must appreciate against the euro relative to its euro central rate, and the other outsider currency must depreciate.

Treaty, this is a nonissue; the country should become a member, unless the Treaty is changed (or other convergence conditions are also made the object of discussion). A country not wishing to join the monetary union, however, should not be required to join the exchange-rate arrangement. Alternatively, if it decides to join in order to leave open the possibility of entering the monetary union at a later time, it should be allowed to opt for the widest possible band.

The other side of the question is whether a country wishing to join the new EMS can be denied membership in it. The answer must be no. If membership in the exchange-rate arrangement is compulsory for admission to the monetary union, no EU partner can be denied *a priori* the possibility of complying with one of the conditions set forth in the Treaty. If a country has a bad record, its currency should be assigned the widest band; if its record does not improve, the correct and legitimate sanction is the suspension of intervention when its currency comes under attack. This leads to a more contentious issue.

Interventions and Conditionality

There can be no objection in principle to granting the ECB the right to invoke a suspension clause and the power to initiate the realignment procedure. This decision, however, cannot be left to arbitrary discretion. It should be made contingent, and should be known to be contingent, upon the acknowledged or potential realization of conditions incompatible with further support of the existing parity. At the moment, the prevailing view seems to be that intervention can be suspended if and when the ECB judges that intervention would conflict with the ECB's ability to control the money supply and, thus, with the objective of price stability.

If support is made dependent only on the ECB's evaluation of the monetary effects of intervention, markets will always win the day when attacking a currency. Because there is practically no limit to the capital that can be mobilized, speculative pressure can always be raised to the point the ECB considers to be the limit beyond which further support would cause loss of control over monetary conditions in the euro area. The prescription of asymmetric sterilization, according to which the ECB should sterilize its interventions, whereas the national central bank whose currency is under attack should not, is an illusory remedy, because full sterilization becomes impossible beyond a certain level.

But is there an alternative? The answer is no, in the case of an ordinary exchange-rate agreement between the currencies of countries whose economic policies are not subject to external supervision and control. It is yes, if the participants explicitly submit themselves to pre-set conditionality, as the signers of the Maastricht Treaty have done. In the latter case, the agreement is, as noted, a bridge to the single currency. Entering into it signals a willingness to fulfill the conditions for admission to monetary union. The conditions are spelled out in the Treaty, and a time path of convergence can be defined for each partici-pating outsider. The explicit rule for intervention can then be the following: compliance with the convergence program will entitle the outsider's currency to *unlimited* support; unjustified underperformance will lead to withdrawal of support when the currency is attacked.

This rule is superior in at least two respects to a suspension clause based on an appraisal of the domestic monetary consequences of intervention. First, because it is explicitly based on the monitoring and evaluation of the participant's record defined in terms of the domestic fundamentals identified by the Treaty, it protects the performing outsider against the potential effects of unwarranted speculative shocks. This is important, because it is not true that weak fundamentals are always at the root of speculative attacks. Note, for example, the effects on peripheral European currencies of the episodes of "flight to quality" triggered by external crises affecting the rate between deutsche marks and dollars. Second, this rule would allow the ECB to intervene less, rather than compelling it to intervene more. An outsider's measured underperformance would exempt the ECB from its commitment. This rule, moreover, would make it less likely that the currency of a per-forming country would come under attack, once the markets are aware that the ECB's commitment would be, in that case, unlimited. The case of the French franc in the turbulent period following the 1992 crisis is an example. The implementation of this rule, however, would require a procedure for the definition and the monitoring of the outsiders' convergence programs. This raises a delicate institutional issue.

Institutional Problems

As noted above, it is not easy to find a legal basis in the Treaty for a new exchange-rate arrangement. It is suggested that the arrangement should originate in a European Council resolution and in an agreement between the ECB and the national central banks, as was the case with the EMS. The Council resolution of December 5, 1978, however, was precise in defining all the features of the EMS, and the central banks' agreement was confined to describing its operating procedures follow-ing the Council's instructions. It is highly likely now, partly in view of the Treaty provisions, that the Council will take the lead, but the

61

essence of the arrangement will be defined by the agreement between the ECB and the other central banks.

This would be an obstacle to having an intervention rule based on conditionality, as suggested above. The definition of a convergence program and the assessment of a country's performance under that program cannot be the task of an independent (and unaccountable) ECB; these properly belong to other EU bodies, such as the ECOFIN Council and the Economic and Financial Committee, although the ECB and the Commission would have advisory and reporting roles. The problem would not arise if the suspension clause were triggered by an appraisal of the effects of intervention on monetary conditions in an area that clearly falls within the ECB's competence. Under the first and more desirable alternative, the design of the new arrangement should provide for a division of tasks between the Council and the ECB. To make this compatible with the Treaty, it may be necessary to extend to EU currencies the provisions of Article 109 of the Treaty, empowering the Council to conclude exchange-rate agreements for the euro.

5 Conclusions

An exchange-rate arrangement between the euro and the outsider currencies is necessary both to keep the door of the monetary union open to countries unable to join in 1999 and to protect those that will join immediately from unwarranted appreciation of the euro. This principle was accepted in Verona, but most of the work to accomplish it still remains to be done. The difficult task ahead is to reconcile two seemingly conflicting requirements: to ensure to the deserving outsider a safe route toward joining the monetary union, sheltered from the destabilizing effects of market turbulence while preserving the ECB's freedom to pursue its objective of price stability. I have argued that a sensible way to strike an acceptable compromise must rely on explicit conditionality, imposed upon and accepted by the participants and based on an assessment of the extent and the speed of convergence. An attempt to tilt the balance toward the second requirement would produce an intrinsically unstable system. This would happen if the decision to provide or withdraw support were left to the ECB's discretionary judgment of the effects on monetary conditions in the euro area, instead of being taken with reference to a transparent benchmark, such as a country's compliance with a convergence program. This kind of arrangement would offer no benefit to the ECB in terms of limiting the amount of intervention and could cause irretrievable damage to an outsider by delaying its prospects of entry.[8] The behavior of the insiders toward the outsiders would then very much resemble that of the Sampson of *Romeo and Juliet* (in Verona):

ABRAHAM: Do you bite your thumb at us, sir?

SAMPSON: Is the law on our side if I say ay?

GREGORY: No

SAMPSON: No, sir, I do not bite my thumb at you, sir; but I bite my thumb, sir.

[8] The exchange-rate criterion requires that the country should not have devalued its currency on its own initiative in the two years prior to seeking admission; if a speculative attack and withdrawal of support leads to devaluation, who can judge, and how, whose initiative it was?

INTERPRETING THE EXCHANGE-RATE CRITERION

Niels Thygesen

One of the several difficult issues facing the completion of the process of European monetary union is the reinterpretation of the convergence criteria in the Maastricht Treaty under circumstances that differ considerably from those prevailing or foreseeable at the Treaty's signing in early 1992. The most visible change in the environment is the near suspension of the rules of the European Monetary System (EMS) that occurred when the traditional narrow margins requiring intervention in exchange markets were dramatically widened in August 1993. Although the European countries have on the whole succeeded in limiting exchange-rate fluctuations over the past few years, the weakening of the EMS forces a rethinking of the way in which the exchange-rate criterion can be applied constructively in 1998.

Many official statements have recently confirmed that the third and final stage of Europe's monetary union will start on January 1, 1999, the final date set by the Maastricht Treaty. The number of countries that will be able to meet the convergence criteria sufficiently well to be admitted, however, remains in doubt. This uncertainty results in part from the fact that some of the criteria are ambiguous; the reference values for the maximum permissible ratios of public-sector deficits and debt to GDP, for example, have always been subject to interpretation. Since 1993, however, the exchange-rate criterion in Article 109j has also become imprecise—to say the least—and officials have seemed quite content to allow the ambiguity to persist.

According to the Treaty, a country is required to have observed the "normal fluctuations margins" for exchange rates in the EMS for at least two years prior to being declared ready to lock its currency irrevocably. In addition, the candidate country should have refrained from devaluing its currency during this period and should have managed it without creating tensions in the EMS.

At the time the Treaty was signed, this criterion seemed relatively straightforward and reasonable. The signatories were encouraged by the growing participation in the EMS (only Greece and Portugal were outside, and Portugal joined two months after the Treaty's signing) and by the ambition of the newcomers to move from temporarily wider

64

margins of ±6 percent to the ±2¼ percent margins that had been the basis of European exchange-rate cooperation not only since the start of the EMS in 1979, but right back to the launching of its predecessor, the "snake," in 1972. After two decades, this method of operation had every claim to be regarded as "normal." One may question, as Peter Kenen (1995b) has, whether past behavior is necessarily a good guide to the future, but it is not surprising, in the light of experience—in particular, the gradual phasing out of exchange-rate realignments in the EMS during the late 1980s and early 1990s—that central bankers and other officials came to regard participation in the narrow-margin EMS as a valuable or even essential apprenticeship for joining a monetary union.

After almost a year of turbulence in European exchange markets, however, the central-bank governors and finance ministers took the dramatic decision on August 1, 1993, to widen the margin of fluctuation to ±15 percent. A first question to ask, then, is how this change has affected the application of the exchange-rate criterion. Although there has been no official answer yet, opinion has moved toward admitting that the present wide margins may be considered as normal, because they apply to all participants in the EMS. Officials have refrained from any formal reinterpretation along these lines, however, because any formal position would require a unanimous decision by the ECOFIN Council in accordance with the procedure outlined in Article 6 of the Protocol on the Convergence Criteria. By leaving themselves some freedom to define what is normal at the time of deciding on participation in the monetary union—now penciled in for early 1998—the officials have removed the potentially fatal impediment to monetary union that a prior return to narrow margins might have presented.

If such a generous reinterpretation of the exchange-rate criterion is adopted in due course, none of the ten present participants in the EMS is likely to be disqualified from joining monetary union because of exchange-rate performance. Seven of the EMS currencies have had unchanged central rates since January 1987, and the three that have been devalued—the Irish punt in 1993 and the Spanish peseta and Portuguese escudo in 1995—seem to have stabilized well before the beginning of the two-year observation period, which must start in 1996. More important, there has been a tendency for the participants to use only a small part of the available fluctuation margin, there being only a 2 to 3 percent spread between the strongest and the weakest currency in recent months. If anything like this performance continues up to the time of decision, officials can conclude, with some satisfaction, that exchange-rate convergence is sufficient. They will be immune to criticism of their generous interpretation of the formal criterion, because *de facto* stability will have been adequately demonstrated.

The difficult issue today arises primarily in deciding what should be required of the five countries that are not currently participating in the EMS: Finland, Greece, Italy, Sweden, and the United Kingdom. Prior to the autumn of 1992, four of these countries were either in the EMS (Italy, the United Kingdom) or in a unilateral pegging arrangement to the ECU (Sweden, Finland).[1] Official and academic opinion in all four countries has since swung from general support for fixed-but-adjustable exchange rates toward rejection of any such commitment prior to eventual participation in monetary union. Those who manned the currencies' defenses during the 1992–93 speculative attacks have lost influence, and in some cases, their positions. There is a tendency to say, at least in Sweden and the United Kingdom, that the adoption of national inflation targets fully consistent with the objective of the prospective, and later actual, participation in monetary union should be an adequate alternative to an exchange-rate commitment. Recent academic contributions, notably by Persson and Tabellini (1996), have even argued for the superiority of inflation targets over exchange-rate targets.

In view of the continuing modest inflation in most of the EU countries with floating exchange rates, and the greater stability of their exchange rates in the recent period, this change of mood leads the present nonparticipants in the EMS to deemphasize the relevance of reentry into the EMS to their eventual eligibility for membership in the monetary union. They may now prefer to stay outside the EMS and have their credentials evaluated *ex post*, that is, by an examination in early 1998 of the actual degree of stability of their exchange rates compared to that of the EMS participants.

Should the EMS participants accept this further erosion of the interpretation of the exchange-rate criterion or should they insist that participation in the existing loose EMS remain a minimal requirement for fulfilling the exchange-rate criterion of the Treaty? Despite the political expediency of leaving this question unanswered for the time being, or of accepting the position that *ex post* stability may be good enough, there are several reasons for the EMS participants to insist on reentry into the monetary system as a minimum requirement for

---

[1] Greece has never participated in the EMS and is an unlikely candidate for monetary union any time soon. The presence of Greece in the European Union initially gave support to the idea of different speeds of integration. This paper makes no further reference to the specific problems of Greece (or of future members of the European union).

consideration of membership in EMU. One is formal; the others are more substantive.

The formal reason, pointed out most clearly by Spaventa (1996b), is that another convergence criterion in Article 109j already obliges those who want to join the monetary union to keep their inflation rates close to the rates (that is, within 1½ percentage points) of the three most stable economies. From the viewpoint of nominal convergence among the prospective participants in the monetary union, there is, in principle, no need for additional efforts. If a candidate country goes further and sets for itself an inflation target lower than that which is strictly required, it may be applauded, but the achievement cannot substitute for an explicit exchange-rate objective in the framework of the Treaty, which contains—for good reasons based on experience—separate exchange-rate and inflation objectives for the prospective participants.

The first substantive argument in favor of insisting on an exchange-rate objective is that even nearly parallel low-inflation rates cannot assure the degree of exchange-rate stability—nominal or real—to which participants in monetary union aspire. In the global system, swings in exchange rates have been much larger over the medium term than can be explained by the modest observed inflation differentials between Germany, Japan, and the United States since the early 1980s. Within Europe, inflation convergence has remained fairly satisfactory, with twelve EU countries currently meeting the inflation criterion. Yet the exchange rates of currencies not bound by explicit commitments continue to fluctuate much more in the short and medium term than the rates of those currencies that have remained in the EMS. Tough, internationally monitored national inflation targets may help to reduce such fluctuations further, but there is no substitute for an outright exchange-rate objective for bringing stability to exchange rates and for protecting the European Single Market against sudden disruptions of the kind that occurred in 1992–93.

There is a second substantive reason why the prospective participants in monetary union should be reluctant to admit a country that has been unwilling even over a relatively brief transition period to adopt a central rate for its currency and to accept a commitment to keep the market exchange rate within fairly wide margins around it. Having an explicit exchange-rate objective is the most direct method of allowing external considerations to enter into the domestic policy debate. Movements of a currency inside the margins provide valuable information about market perceptions of an economy's performance. Without a framework comprising a central rate and the intervention margins associated with it, such movements will be ambiguous with respect to the implications for corrective policy actions. Comparing the performance of EMS currencies (and of the authorities managing them) has provided countries participating in the system with valuable incentives to adjust that are not present to the same degree in a floating-rate system. In that sense, temporary participation in an EMS arrangement remains an important period of apprenticeship for countries wishing to enter the monetary union—perhaps particularly for those that have had only a brief and unhappy association with the system in the past, such as Finland, Sweden, and the United Kingdom.

A third substantive argument can be advanced for insisting on EMS participation for those currently outside it. Agreeing on a central rate for a currency entering the EMS—and one can expect such a rate to be chosen only after long and careful discussion among the present participants and the entrant—is itself a valuable exercise in two respects: (1) the central rate becomes a point of reference in both stabilizing market expectations and providing a focus for monitoring subsequent performance, and (2) a central rate will facilitate the choice of the conversion rate at which the entering currency will be converted into the future single currency, the euro, on January 1, 1999. These two points deserve further discussion.

In a system with wide fluctuation margins, such as the present EMS, the most important aspect of joining is the announcement of the central rate that both the entrant and its partners regard as an equilibrium rate sustainable for a lengthy period. From this perspective, the additional credibility afforded by obligations to intervene at the distant margins is of only secondary importance. If the new currency enters an EMS marked by anything like the present underutilization of the fluctuation margins, the important interventions will be intramarginal. They will show whether the newcomer is able to stabilize its exchange rate well within the formal margins through its own and its partners' intervention and through domestic monetary adjustments. Consider the so-called Basle-Nyborg Agreement of September 1987, which defined the balance among the three instruments in the short-term defense of a currency— movements inside the fluctuation margins, interventions, and changes in the domestic short-term interest rates of the country whose currency is under speculative attack. If the agreement were revised today, it would have to take into account the massive change in the EMS brought about by the wider margins. A revised agreement would have to devote (even) more attention to rules for intramarginal interventions and their interaction with domestic monetary adjustments, because the 1992–93 crises revealed that countries differed greatly in their views about the order in which the instruments were to be used. France relied heavily on sterilized interventions and proved unwilling to raise domestic interest rates, whereas Germany would have preferred France do just the opposite.

It is highly doubtful that a revised Basle-Nyborg Agreement could be negotiated today. Even if that proved possible, the new understanding would grant considerable discretion to the authorities of countries whose currencies are not under attack. All of this reinforces the point that the main element inherent in entry into the EMS is the agreement on the central rate rather than on interventions that are either mandatory, but at remote margins, or are intramarginal and discretionary.

As to whether a central rate will facilitate the choice of the conversion rate, there is no presumption that the future conversion rates for the currencies participating in the EMS and joining monetary union will necessarily coincide with the central rate, although such a choice will appear increasingly likely if the present high degree of stability in the EMS persists. Even if some currencies are converted into the euro at rates different from present central rates, it will be helpful to start from the well-tested sustainability of such rates rather than to have to devise at much shorter notice additional principles for setting the conversion rates on December 31, 1998, for those monetary-union participants that do not yet have a central rate. Such a perspective on the importance of the central rate over a longer term will raise the stakes for those currently outside the EMS, because they will realize that they could be making a permanent choice rather than simply choosing a rate for a relatively brief transition period. If they see this as a deterrent to their participation in the EMS, they might be assured that although the use of the central rate to set the future conversion rate will be the rule, another rate may be chosen in exceptional cases.

This argument suggests that it might be sufficient from an economic point of view to require those outside the EMS to negotiate central rates for their currencies soon, without necessarily committing themselves to defending particular intervention rates (see Thygesen, 1994, for a discussion of targets without zones). But this would hardly be consistent with the requirement of the Treaty that countries should observe the normal EMS margins. Given the width of these margins, it is unrealistic for the present nonparticipants to argue that such a commitment would, in itself, encourage speculative attacks to test the resolve of the authorities; with the painful experience of 1992–93 still fresh in their minds, however, they have nevertheless tended to claim that it would. If there is, objectively, little risk of such destabilizing speculation, it seems reasonable for the EMS participants to insist on the announcement not only of central rates, but also of intervention margins for the newcomers.

To summarize, there are, on balance, sound arguments for obliging countries that want to join the monetary union to enter the EMS. In fact, a clear statement to this effect needs to be made soon, before coming too close to the time in early 1998 when it will be decided which countries will participate in monetary union. We are already less than two years from this point of decision. There is thus a strong case for telling countries that do not currently participate in the EMS that unless they join the present system sometime soon, that is, in 1996, the earliest date at which they may be considered eligible for monetary union will be two years after they join either the EMS, if prior to January 1, 1999, or whatever successor arrangement may be designed after the demise of the EMS. A logical minimum variant of such an arrangement would consist in setting a central euro rate for currencies entering the system, with margins of 7½ percent on either side; this would leave the same scope for fluctuations between any two currencies outside the monetary union as exists today. There is a close analogy in this to the response adopted by the Europeans to the Smithsonian Agreement of December 1971, which enlarged fluctuation margins vis-à-vis the U.S. dollar. The Europeans did not want a widening of the margins between their currencies to twice those against the dollar, so they introduced the bilateral parity grid of the snake, by which the maximum distance between the strongest and the weakest currency was set at only half that of the maximum range set by the Smithsonian Agreement. As Europe now moves back from a bilateral parity grid to a system in which nonparticipants in monetary union will peg to the euro, it would be advisable to narrow the fluctuation margins to prevent a *de facto* widening of bilateral variability between currencies pegged to the euro. A statement to this effect by the group of countries likely to join monetary union would constitute an enforceable interpretation of the exchange-rate criterion.

At least one nonparticipant in the EMS, the United Kingdom, would be unlikely to sign such a statement. It is well known that an EMS-like arrangement for sterling is even less popular in the United Kingdom than participation in the monetary union itself. The present U.K. government can hardly be expected to rejoin the EMS to preserve the option of participating at the start in a monetary union it may not ever want to join. Yet the increasing likelihood of a referendum to take such a decision and the apparent U.K. inclination to adopt a wait-and-see attitude until a first group has moved ahead and made an initial success of monetary union, suggests that the delay in participation may not pose insurmountable problems for subsequent entry.

Because the United Kingdom is exempt from the general obligation to join monetary union even when the convergence criteria are fully met, its status relative to the other current nonparticipants in the EMS is unique. This may imply, as Britain suggests, that an opportunity for the United Kingdom to join monetary union without prior participation in the EMS would not necessarily create a precedent for the other countries currently outside the system. It should be noted, however, that the only other country with a right to opt out of monetary union, Denmark, is a participant in the EMS and has indicated an interest in maintaining the tightest possible exchange-rate arrangement with the euro that will be available after January 1, 1999.

It is more likely, although not certain, that the three other current nonparticipants in the EMS—Finland, Italy, and Sweden—will decide to join the EMS if membership is necessary to preserve access to monetary union. But it should not be overlooked that any confirmation of the suggested interpretation of the exchange-rate criterion would at the same time give countries outside the EMS a ready-made opt-out from monetary union that they do not currently have: by simply refusing to join the EMS and its successor arrangement, they would fail to qualify for monetary union, even if they have satisfied the other convergence criteria. The stakes are therefore higher than may immediately be apparent. It should also be noted, however, that most of the participants in the monetary union would agree that the proposal is reasonable and that it represents a minimalist interpretation of the Treaty. If some nonparticipants consider it an impediment to joining monetary union, they would be indicating that they are not yet ready for monetary union.

The discussion in this brief essay has focused on the appropriate interpretation of the exchange-rate criterion for those countries that are, in principle, aspiring to join monetary union. The analysis also has implications, however, for the design of the arrangement between the insiders and outsiders after monetary union has started. This subject is dealt with at some length in Thygesen (1996) and in a report by the Centre for European Policy Studies (CEPS) Economic Policy Group (Gros, 1996).

There is no way in which the participants in monetary union can oblige countries that either do not meet the convergence criteria or are politically unwilling to join the union to take part in an exchange-rate arrangement after monetary union begins. If this group is large, proposals should be worked out that give the insiders the right to approve and modify central rates for the currencies of outsiders in return for providing some mutual-support facilities within and at the limits of the wide margins of ±7½ percent around central rates. Arrangements might be differentiated according to the degree of progress made by each outsider in respecting the convergence criteria and by its readiness to subject its monetary policy to the guidelines set by the European Central Bank (ECB). The closer an outsider is to meeting the criteria and the more ready it is to acknowledge the fundamentally asymmetric nature of its monetary relation with the ECB, the bolder the participants in monetary union should be in their offer of support for the outsider's currency. For most current and future outsiders, the fact that participation in the successor arrangement to the EMS will be part of the convergence criteria should be sufficient to induce them to participate in a minimal variant of the successor arrangement of the sort discussed.

REFERENCES

Arrowsmith, John A.A., "Economic and Monetary Union in a Multi-Tier Europe," *National Institute Economic Review*, 152 (May 1995a), pp. 76–96.
———, "Opting Out of Stage 3: Life in the Lower Tier of EMU," London, National Institute of Economic and Social Research, June 1995b, processed.
———, "Economic and Monetary Union: Economic, Financial and Legal Aspects of the Transition to a Single European Currency," written evidence to the Treasury Committee of the House of Commons, January 1996; in Treasury Committee, Eighth Report, *The Prognosis for Stage 3 of Economic and Monetary Union*, HC 283, Vol. 2, HMSO, July 1996, pp. 284–295.
Barber, Lionel, "Brussels Ducks Decision on EMU Requirement," *Financial Times*, December 20, 1995, p. 2.
Barro, Robert J., and Xavier Sala-i-Martin, "World Real Interest Rates," *NBER Macroeconomics Annual* (1991), pp. 5–10.
Bayoumi, Tamim A., and Barry Eichengreen, "Shocking Aspects of European Monetary Integration," in Francisco Torres and Francesco Giavazzi, eds., *Adjustment and Growth in the European Monetary Union*, Cambridge and New York, Cambridge University Press, 1993, pp. 193–229.
Bayoumi, Tamim A., and Paul R. Masson, "Fiscal Flows in the United States and Canada: Lessons for Monetary Union in Europe," CEPR Discussion Paper No. 1057, London, Centre for Economic Policy Research, November 1994.
Bishop, Graham, "The EC's Public Debt Disease: Discipline with Credit Spreads and Cure with Price Stability," *Salomon Brothers Economic and Market Analysis*, London, May 1991; reprinted in Donald E. Fair and Christian de Boissieu, eds., *Fiscal Policy, Taxation, and the Financial System in an Increasingly Integrated Europe*, Financial and Monetary Policy Studies No. 22, Norwell, Mass., and Dordrecht, Kluwer for the Société Universitaire Européene de Recherches Financieres, 1992, pp. 207–234.
———, "Valuing Public Debt in the EC: EMU Benefits versus 'No-Bail-Out' Risks," *Salomon Brothers Economic and Market Analysis*, London, November 1991.
Borgatta, Gino, "La Politica Monetaria nel Sistema Corporativo," in "Dieci Anni di Economia Fascista: 1926–1035," *Annali de Economia*, Vol. 12, Padua, Cedam, 1936.
Buiter, Willem H., Giancarlo Corsetti, and Nouriel Roubini, "Sense and Nonsense in the Treaty of Maastricht," *Economic Policy*, 16 (April 1993), pp. 57–100.
Capie, Forrest, Charles Goodhart, Stanley Fischer, and Norbert Schnadt, *The Future of Central Banking: The Tercentenary Symposium of the Bank of England*, Cambridge, New York, and Melbourne, Cambridge University Press, 1994.

Commission of the European Communities (Commission), *Report on Convergence in the European Union in 1995*, Brussels, Commission of the European Communities, November 1995.

De Grauwe, Paul, *The Economics of Monetary Integration*, 2nd rev. ed., Oxford and New York, Oxford University Press, 1994a.

———, "Towards EMU without the EMS," *Economic Policy*, 18 (April 1994b), pp. 149–174.

———, "The Economics of Convergence towards Monetary Union in Europe," CEPR Discussion Paper No. 1213, London, Centre for Economic Policy Research, July 1995.

De Grauwe, Paul, and Wim Vanhaverbeke, "Is Europe an Optimum Currency Area? Evidence from Regional Data," in Paul R. Masson and Mark P. Taylor, eds., *Policy Issues in the Operation of Currency Unions*, Cambridge, Cambridge University Press, 1993, pp. 111–129.

Dewatripont, Mathias, et al., "Flexible Integration: Towards a More Effective and Democratic Europe," *Monitoring European Integration*, 6, London, Centre for Economic Policy Research, 1995.

Eichengreen, Barry, and Jürgen von Hagen, "Fiscal Policy and Monetary Union: Federalism, Fiscal Restrictions and the No-Bailout Rule," CEPR Discussion Paper No. 1247, London, Centre for Economic Policy Research, September 1995.

European Monetary Institute (EMI), *Annual Report 1994*, Frankfurt, European Monetary Institute, April 1995a.

———, *Progress towards Convergence*, Frankfurt, European Monetary Institute, November 1995b.

Feldstein, Martin, and Charles Horioka, "Domestic Saving and International Capital Flows," *Economic Journal* (London), 90 (June 1980), pp. 314–329.

Goodhart, Charles A.E., *Money, Information, and Uncertainty*, 2nd ed., Cambridge, Mass., MIT Press, 1989.

———, *The Central Bank and the Financial System*, Hounds Mills, Basingstoke, Macmillan, 1995.

———, *The Transition to EMU*, Second Annual Lecture, Scottish Economic Society and Royal Bank of Scotland, January 1996; reprinted in *Scottish Journal of Political Economy*, 43 (August 1996), pp. 241–257.

Gros, Daniel, "Towards a Credible Excessive Deficits Procedure," CEPS Working Document No. 95, Brussels, Centre for European Policy Studies, April 1995a.

———, "Self-Fulfilling Public Debt Crises," Brussels, Centre for European Policy Studies, May 1995b, processed.

———, "Towards Economic and Monetary Union: Problems and Prospects," CEPS Paper No. 65, Brussels, Centre for European Policy Studies, January 1996.

Gros, Daniel, and Niels Thygesen, *European Monetary Integration: From the European Monetary System to European Monetary Union*, London, Longman; New York, St. Martin's, 1992.

Helbling, Thomas, and Robert Wescott, "The Global Real Interest Rate," in International Monetary Fund, *World Economic and Financial Surveys*, Washington, D.C., International Monetary Fund, September 1995, pp. 83–99.

Johnson, Christopher, "The New Wide-Band Exchange-Rate Mechanism: Rules versus Discretion in a Target Zone," International Monetary Fund Seminar Paper, Washington, D.C., International Monetary Fund, July 1994, processed.

Kenen, Peter B., "The Theory of Optimum Currency Areas: An Eclectic View," in Robert A. Mundell and Alexander K. Swoboda, eds., *Monetary Problems of the International Economy*, Chicago and London, University of Chicago Press, 1969, pp. 41–60.

———, "Can the EMU Fly?" in *EMU Prospects*, Occasional Paper No. 50, Washington, D.C., Group of Thirty, 1995a, pp. 19–33.

———, *Economic and Monetary Union in Europe: Moving beyond Maastricht*, Cambridge and New York, Cambridge University Press, 1995b.

———, "Hazards on the Road to the Third Stage of Economic and Monetary Union," paper prepared for the Forum for US-EC Legal-Economic Affairs, Session on Issues of Governance in the European Community, London, September 1995c.

McKinnon, Ronald I., "Optimum Currency Areas," *American Economic Review*, 53 (September 1963), pp. 717–724.

Moesen, Wim, and Paul Van Rompuy, "The Growth of Government Size and Fiscal Decentralization," paper prepared for the International Institute of Public Finance Congress in Brussels, August 1990.

Mundell, Robert A., "A Theory of Optimum Currency Areas," *American Economic Review*, 51 (September 1961), pp. 657–664.

Neumann, Manfred J.M., and Jürgen von Hagen, "Real Exchange Rates within and between Currency Areas: How Far Away is EMU?" *Review of Economics and Statistics*, 76 (May 1994), pp. 236–244.

Obstfeld, Maurice, "International Capital Mobility in the 1990s," National Bureau of Economic Research Working Paper No. 4534, Cambridge, Mass., National Bureau of Economic Research, November 1993.

Persson, Torsten, and Guido Tabellini, "Monetary Cohabitation in Europe," National Bureau of Economic Research Working Paper No. 5532, Cambridge, Mass., National Bureau of Economic Research, April 1996.

Richards, O. Paul, "EMU: Unresolved Issues Relating to Stage 3," in Ian D. Davidson and Christopher T. Taylor, eds., *European Monetary Union: The Kingsdown Enquiry*, London, Macmillan, 1995, pp. 332–350.

Spaventa, Luigi, "A Survey of the Issues," paper presented at the Centre for Economic Policy Research/Banca Nazionale del Lavoro Conference in Rome, February 26, 1996a.

———, "Out in the Cold? Outsiders and Insiders in 1999: Feasible and Unfeasible Options," CEPR Discussion Paper No. 1379, London, Centre for Economic Policy Research, April 1996b.

75

Tavlas, George, "The Theory of Monetary Integration," *Open Economies Review*, 5 (March 1994), pp. 211–230.

Taylor, Christopher T., "Exchange Rate Arrangements for a Multi-Speed Europe," EUI Working Paper No. 95/35, Florence, European University Institute, Robert Schuman Centre, 1995.

Thygesen, Niels, "Études Critiques des Zones Cibles et Réflexions sur l'Expérience du SME," in Thierry Walrafen, ed., *Bretton Woods—Mélanges pour un Cinquantenaire*, Paris, Le Monde, 1994, pp. 245–262.

———, "The Prospects for EMU by 1999—and Reflections on Arrangements for the Outsiders," paper presented at the Centre for Economic Policy Research/Banca Nazionale del Lavoro Conference in Rome, February 26, 1996.

Wyplosz, Charles, "An EMS for Both 'Ins' and 'Outs': The Contractual and Conditional Approach," paper presented at the Centre for Economic Policy Research/Banca Nazionale del Lavoro Conference in Rome, February 26, 1996; summarized in *Swiss Political Science Review*, 2 (Spring 1996), pp. 178–183.

PUBLICATIONS OF THE
INTERNATIONAL FINANCE SECTION

Notice to Contributors

The International Finance Section publishes papers in four series: ESSAYS IN INTERNATIONAL FINANCE, PRINCETON STUDIES IN INTERNATIONAL FINANCE, and SPECIAL PAPERS IN INTERNATIONAL ECONOMICS contain new work not published elsewhere. REPRINTS IN INTERNATIONAL FINANCE reproduce journal articles previously published by Princeton faculty members associated with the Section. The Section welcomes the submission of manuscripts for publication under the following guidelines:

ESSAYS are meant to disseminate new views about international financial matters and should be accessible to well-informed nonspecialists as well as to professional economists. Technical terms, tables, and charts should be used sparingly; mathematics should be avoided.

STUDIES are devoted to new research on international finance, with preference given to empirical work. They should be comparable in originality and technical proficiency to papers published in leading economic journals. They should be of medium length, longer than a journal article but shorter than a book.

SPECIAL PAPERS are surveys of research on particular topics and should be suitable for use in undergraduate courses. They may be concerned with international trade as well as international finance. They should also be of medium length.

Manuscripts should be submitted in triplicate, typed single sided and double spaced throughout on 8½ by 11 white bond paper. Publication can be expedited if manuscripts are computer keyboarded in WordPerfect 5.1 or a compatible program. Additional instructions and a style guide are available from the Section.

How to Obtain Publications

The Section's publications are distributed free of charge to college, university, and public libraries and to nongovernmental, nonprofit research institutions. Eligible institutions may ask to be placed on the Section's permanent mailing list.

Individuals and institutions not qualifying for free distribution may receive all publications for the calendar year for a subscription fee of $40.00. Late subscribers will receive all back issues for the year during which they subscribe. Subscribers should notify the Section promptly of any change in address, giving the old address as well as the new.

Publications may be ordered individually, with payment made in advance. ESSAYS and REPRINTS cost $8.00 each; STUDIES and SPECIAL PAPERS cost $11.00. An additional $1.50 should be sent for postage and handling within the United States, Canada, and Mexico; $1.75 should be added for surface delivery outside the region.

All payments must be made in U.S. dollars. Subscription fees and charges for single issues will be waived for organizations and individuals in countries where foreign-exchange regulations prohibit dollar payments.

Please address all correspondence, submissions, and orders to:

International Finance Section
Department of Economics, Fisher Hall
Princeton University
Princeton, New Jersey 08544-1021

List of Recent Publications

A complete list of publications may be obtained from the International Finance Section.

ESSAYS IN INTERNATIONAL FINANCE

165. Rudiger Dornbusch, *Inflation, Exchange Rates, and Stabilization.* (October 1986)
166. John Spraos, *IMF Conditionality: Ineffectual, Inefficient, Mistargeted.* (December 1986)
167. Rainer Stefano Masera, *An Increasing Role for the ECU: A Character in Search of a Script.* (June 1987)
168. Paul Mosley, *Conditionality as Bargaining Process: Structural-Adjustment Lending, 1980-86.* (October 1987)
169. Paul A. Volcker, Ralph C. Bryant, Leonhard Gleske, Gottfried Haberler, Alexandre Lamfalussy, Shijuro Ogata, Jesús Silva-Herzog, Ross M. Starr, James Tobin, and Robert Triffin, *International Monetary Cooperation: Essays in Honor of Henry C. Wallich.* (December 1987)
170. Shafiqul Islam, *The Dollar and the Policy-Performance-Confidence Mix.* (July 1988)
171. James M. Boughton, *The Monetary Approach to Exchange Rates: What Now Remains?* (October 1988)
172. Jack M. Guttentag and Richard M. Herring, *Accounting for Losses On Sovereign Debt: Implications for New Lending.* (May 1989)
173. Benjamin J. Cohen, *Developing-Country Debt: A Middle Way.* (May 1989)
174. Jeffrey D. Sachs, *New Approaches to the Latin American Debt Crisis.* (July 1989)
175. C. David Finch, *The IMF: The Record and the Prospect.* (September 1989)
176. Graham Bird, *Loan-Loss Provisions and Third-World Debt.* (November 1989)
177. Ronald Findlay, *The "Triangular Trade" and the Atlantic Economy of the Eighteenth Century: A Simple General-Equilibrium Model.* (March 1990)
178. Alberto Giovannini, *The Transition to European Monetary Union.* (November 1990)
179. Michael L. Mussa, *Exchange Rates in Theory and in Reality.* (December 1990)
180. Warren L. Coats, Jr., Reinhard W. Furstenberg, and Peter Isard, *The SDR System and the Issue of Resource Transfers.* (December 1990)
181. George S. Tavlas, *On the International Use of Currencies: The Case of the Deutsche Mark.* (March 1991)
182. Tommaso Padoa-Schioppa, ed., with Michael Emerson, Kumiharu Shigehara, and Richard Portes, *Europe After 1992: Three Essays.* (May 1991)
183. Michael Bruno, *High Inflation and the Nominal Anchors of an Open Economy.* (June 1991)
184. Jacques J. Polak, *The Changing Nature of IMF Conditionality.* (September 1991)
185. Ethan B. Kapstein, *Supervising International Banks: Origins and Implications of the Basle Accord.* (December 1991)
186. Alessandro Giustiniani, Francesco Papadia, and Daniela Porciani, *Growth and Catch-Up in Central and Eastern Europe: Macroeconomic Effects on Western Countries.* (April 1992)

187. Michele Fratianni, Jürgen von Hagen, and Christopher Waller, *The Maastricht Way to EMU*. (June 1992)

188. Pierre-Richard Agénor, *Parallel Currency Markets in Developing Countries: Theory, Evidence, and Policy Implications*. (November 1992)

189. Beatriz Armendariz de Aghion and John Williamson, *The G-7's Joint-and-Several Blunder*. (April 1993)

190. Paul Krugman, *What Do We Need to Know About the International Monetary System?* (July 1993)

191. Peter M. Garber and Michael G. Spencer, *The Dissolution of the Austro-Hungarian Empire: Lessons for Currency Reform*. (February 1994)

192. Raymond F. Mikesell, *The Bretton Woods Debates: A Memoir*. (March 1994)

193. Graham Bird, *Economic Assistance to Low-Income Countries: Should the Link be Resurrected?* (July 1994)

194. Lorenzo Bini-Smaghi, Tommaso Padoa-Schioppa, and Francesco Papadia, *The Transition to EMU in the Maastricht Treaty*. (November 1994)

195. Ariel Buira, *Reflections on the International Monetary System*. (January 1995)

196. Shinji Takagi, *From Recipient to Donor: Japan's Official Aid Flows, 1945 to 1990 and Beyond*. (March 1995)

197. Patrick Conway, *Currency Proliferation: The Monetary Legacy of the Soviet Union*. (June 1995)

198. Barry Eichengreen, *A More Perfect Union? The Logic of Economic Integration*. (June 1996)

199. Peter B. Kenen, ed., with John Arrowsmith, Paul De Grauwe, Charles A. E. Goodhart, Daniel Gros, Luigi Spaventa, and Niels Thygesen, *Making EMU Happen—Problems and Proposals: A Symposium*. (August 1996)

PRINCETON STUDIES IN INTERNATIONAL FINANCE

58. John T. Cuddington, *Capital Flight: Estimates, Issues, and Explanations*. (December 1986)

59. Vincent P. Crawford, *International Lending, Long-Term Credit Relationships, and Dynamic Contract Theory*. (March 1987)

60. Thorvaldur Gylfason, *Credit Policy and Economic Activity in Developing Countries with IMF Stabilization Programs*. (August 1987)

61. Stephen A. Schuker, *American "Reparations" to Germany, 1919-33: Implications for the Third-World Debt Crisis*. (July 1988)

62. Steven B. Kamin, *Devaluation, External Balance, and Macroeconomic Performance: A Look at the Numbers*. (August 1988)

63. Jacob A. Frenkel and Assaf Razin, *Spending, Taxes, and Deficits: International-Intertemporal Approach*. (December 1988)

64. Jeffrey A. Frankel, *Obstacles to International Macroeconomic Policy Coordination*. (December 1988)

65. Peter Hooper and Catherine L. Mann, *The Emergence and Persistence of the U.S. External Imbalance, 1980-87*. (October 1989)

66. Helmut Reisen, *Public Debt, External Competitiveness, and Fiscal Discipline in Developing Countries*. (November 1989)

67. Victor Argy, Warwick McKibbin, and Eric Siegloff, *Exchange-Rate Regimes for a Small Economy in a Multi-Country World*. (December 1989)
68. Mark Gersovitz and Christina H. Paxson, *The Economies of Africa and the Prices of Their Exports*. (October 1990)
69. Felipe Larraín and Andrés Velasco, *Can Swaps Solve the Debt Crisis? Lessons from the Chilean Experience*. (November 1990)
70. Kaushik Basu, *The International Debt Problem, Credit Rationing and Loan Pushing: Theory and Experience*. (October 1991)
71. Daniel Gros and Alfred Steinherr, *Economic Reform in the Soviet Union: Pas de Deux between Disintegration and Macroeconomic Destabilization*. (November 1991)
72. George M. von Furstenberg and Joseph P. Daniels, *Economic Summit Declarations, 1975-1989: Examining the Written Record of International Cooperation*. (February 1992)
73. Ishac Diwan and Dani Rodrik, *External Debt, Adjustment, and Burden Sharing: A Unified Framework*. (November 1992)
74. Barry Eichengreen, *Should the Maastricht Treaty Be Saved?* (December 1992)
75. Adam Klug, *The German Buybacks, 1932-1939: A Cure for Overhang?* (November 1993)
76. Tamim Bayoumi and Barry Eichengreen, *One Money or Many? Analyzing the Prospects for Monetary Unification in Various Parts of the World*. (September 1994)
77. Edward E. Leamer, *The Heckscher-Ohlin Model in Theory and Practice*. (February 1995)
78. Thorvaldur Gylfason, *The Macroeconomics of European Agriculture*. (May 1995)
79. Angus S. Deaton and Ronald I. Miller, *International Commodity Prices, Macroeconomic Performance, and Politics in Sub-Saharan Africa*. (December 1995)
80. Chander Kant, *Foreign Direct Investment and Capital Flight*. (April 1996)

SPECIAL PAPERS IN INTERNATIONAL ECONOMICS

16. Elhanan Helpman, *Monopolistic Competition in Trade Theory*. (June 1990)
17. Richard Pomfret, *International Trade Policy with Imperfect Competition*. (August 1992)
18. Hali J. Edison, *The Effectiveness of Central-Bank Intervention: A Survey of the Literature After 1982*. (July 1993)
19. Sylvester W.C. Eijffinger and Jakob de Haan, *The Political Economy of Central-Bank Independence*. (May 1996)

REPRINTS IN INTERNATIONAL FINANCE

27. Peter B. Kenen, *Transitional Arrangements for Trade and Payments Among the CMEA Countries*; reprinted from *International Monetary Fund Staff Papers* 38 (2), 1991. (July 1991)
28. Peter B. Kenen, *Ways to Reform Exchange-Rate Arrangements*; reprinted from *Bretton Woods: Looking to the Future*, 1994. (November 1994)